Final Examination Paper 15

PUBLIC SECTOR ORGANISATION AND FINANCIAL CONTROL

Published March 1992 by Financial Training Courses, Publishing and Distance Learning, 151 Freston Road, London W10 6TH

ISBN 1 85179 409 3

Past examination questions have been reproduced by kind permission of the Association of Accounting Technicians.

Answers have been prepared by our team of specialist authors.

Printed in England.

27160

CONTENTS

INTRODUCTION

This Revision Pack provides students with sufficient practice at questions to ensure confidence in the exam. The aim is to cover all areas of the syllabus and give a balanced range of questions, most of which are from recent past exams.

HOW TO USE THIS REVISION PACK

The Revision Pack is split into two sections: a bank of questions with answers and a mock exam. The questions are organised by topic to ensure you cannot forget any of the areas on which you may be examined.

Do questions without reference to your notes and time yourself strictly; it is better to know your weaknesses now than on the day itself! Nothing is more infuriating than wasting months of hard work by mistiming an answer in the exam.

The model answers are there to help you; learn from their structure and content and check your answers against them carefully.

The Revision Pack ends with a mock exam which, if attempted under exam conditions, is an excellent opportunity to develop your exam technique.

STUDENTS ENROLLING ON REVISION COURSES

This Revision Pack provides the material for the revision course. Students enrolling on these courses should not use the questions in the Pack before attending the course.

FORMAT OF THE EXAMINATION

The paper will comprise **six** questions of which you have to attempt **four**. Two of the six questions will be mini–case studies.

SYLLABUS

Aims

To develop an understanding of the constitution of public sector organisations and the legislative and economic context within which they operate, and of the need for and the nature of financial management in the public sector.

Organisation

15%   **The organisation** (specific type of public sector organisation): functions and legislative authority; constitutional provisions; administrative and financial relationships with other parts of the public sector.

15%   **Finance:** main areas of expenditure and sources of capital and revenue finance.

15%   **Management – policy and structure:** the legislative and executive role in management; divisions of executive responsibility; communications; personnel management; the place of the finance function in management.

Financial control

20%   **Financial control:** control systems of capital and revenue expenditure; cash and credit income; financial standing orders and regulations; tendering and purchasing; contracts and payment of final accounts; control of stores and equipment.

20%   **Financial procedures:** basic forms of income and expenditure analysis including allocation of centralised common services; payment procedures for creditors and employees; accounting for cash, banking and giro services; security of cash; banking arrangements.

15%   **Financial management:** organisation of financial services; organisation and methods of financing of capital and revenue expenditure; investment appraisal; borrowing methods; management of funds; revenue and capital accounts relating to the main types of funds operated within the various public sector organisations.

EXAMINERS' COMMENTS AND EXAM TECHNIQUE

What the examiners say

The examiners' reports on the scripts they receive are alarmingly similar every time. The following points are raised again and again; if you avoid the following errors you will already have a head start on other candidates.

(1)   **The standard of handwriting and presentation is low**

Students **are** penalised for this, and you should make every effort to write legibly, label diagrams properly and present your work professionally. The examiner may have up to 3,000 scripts to mark; a badly written scrawl cannot expect the same attention as a well laid out paper.

(2)   **Students do not answer the question**

Examiners know what the question was and are not interested in the extent of your knowledge in other areas. To write a model answer to a different question is a waste of time. 'Candidates should answer the question asked and not the question they would have wished to be asked.'

(3)   **Answers are poorly structured and lack direction**

Always take time to organise your answers and think about the points you need to make. Do not begin writing in the hope that inspiration will strike; it never does and you waste valuable time without gaining any marks.

(4)   **Students include irrelevant facts**

'Quantity does not mean quality' has never been more true. The examiner will see straight through any attempts at padding and you would be better advised to use the time to think of any other **relevant** information.

(5)   **Mere reproduction of learned notes is not enough**

You must be able to apply your knowledge, analyse problems and reach logical conclusions. Examiners are testing more than your memory and will be unimpressed by candidates who have not considered the question critically.

Exam technique

Your success or failure in exams will depend on two things:

(a)   your knowledge;

(b)   your ability to apply that knowledge to situations in the exam (**exam technique**).

Your final revision will consolidate your knowledge, but you must also develop your exam technique.

Never forget the ten basic principles which underlie all exam attempts.

(1)   Read the instructions on the front of the paper indicating which questions to answer.

(2)   Read through the paper.

(3) Consider the order in which you are going to tackle questions. Starting with your best question often gives a boost to your morale.

(4) At the start of each question note down the time at which you must finish that question. **Never go over this time.**

(5) Answer the individual parts of questions in your best order (get the marks you can get).

(6) Lay out answers neatly. Remember around 10% of the marks could be for presentation.

      Remember: Headings
                        Handwriting
                        Good English

(7) Always show your workings somewhere in your answer. If they are on separate sheets, cross reference through to your final answer.

(8) Don't get bogged down in minor parts of questions. If you are stuck, **leave it** and get on with the rest of the question.

(9) Remember if it's a hard question, it is hard for **everybody** so keep going.

(10) Don't panic! You only need around half marks. Passing exams is based on **getting the easy marks** in every question.

Case study questions

Two of the six questions on Paper 15 are mini–case studies. The examiner has made it clear that marks will be awarded for both development and argument as well as the final answer.

Your approach to these questions should be as follows:

–   read through the case study a couple of times to get a feel for the subject–matter;
–   define the problem or issue carefully;
–   set out possible solutions to the problem;
–   demonstrate that you can put foward a feasible course of action.

ANALYSIS OF THE LAST SIX PAPERS

	1989 June	1989 Dec	1990 June	1990 Dec	1991 June	1991 Dec
The organisation	●	●	●	●		●●
Management policy and structure						
– responsibilities		●				
– communication		●				
– staff			●	●	●	
Financial control and management						
– budgets and budgetary control		●				●
– sources of income and grants	●					
– rates/poll tax/ community charge		●		●	●	
– appraisal of capital projects			●	●		●
– finance department roles	●			●		●
– internal funds						
– TIA 1961						
– financial control systems			●	●		●
– internal audit	●	●				
– methods of financing expenditure	●				●	
– tenders				●		
– insurance			●			
Financial procedures						
– cash movements		●			●	
– wages and salaries		●				
– payment for services						
– use of common services			●			
– control accounts and bank reconciliation statements	●				●	
– computer systems					●	

REVISION TOPICS

1   **The organisation**

(a)   Revise the basic structure of the organisation of the public sector. In particular the central government departments, the water industry and the national health service.

(b)   Revise the role of central government and the manner in which central government controls the public sector as a whole.

(c)   Revise the present system that governs the structure of the local authorities. The number of tiers is clearly a current topic and you should be up to date in the matter of the abolition of the metropolitan councils.

(d)   The health service is an important element of the public sector. Ensure that you understand its current structure and the various tiers involved.

(e)   Revise carefully the relationship between central government and public sector organisations.

(f)   Revise the areas where the public authorities cooperate with the other bodies.

2   **Management – policy and structure**

(a)   Revise the essential factors for management: planning, organisation, coordination, etc.

(b)   Revise the difference between line and staff organisations.

(c)   Revise the concepts of coordination, span of control, responsibility and delegation of authority.

(d)   Revise the concept of 'corporate management'.

(e)   Revise the theory and practice of policy making.

(f)   Corporate planning is an important area and you should be aware of its main features.

(g)   Communication is an important area of the syllabus. Revise the basic theory of communication and its practical application to meetings.

(h)   Revise how committees work and how local authorities are governed by committees.

3   **Financial control and management**

This is a central part of the syllabus and you must revise thoroughly the following areas.

(a)   The main areas of revenue expenditure. You should know roughly speaking what percentage of a local authority's expenditure is allocated to the different areas.

(b)   You should be aware of the CIPFA's revised standard form of accounts, including the subjective and objective analysis.

(c) Be aware of the sources of income and, again, the percentage that each area contributes to the total. The revenue support grant is an important element of income and you should be aware of how this operates.

(d) Be aware of how the community charge is calculated.

(e) Capital expenditure is very important for local authorities. Be aware of the definition of capital and revenue expenditure.

(f) Make sure that you understand how capital projects are appraised.

(g) Be aware of the various methods of financing capital expenditure.

(h) Be able to draw up a typical structure for a finance department and understand the roles of each of the offices and departments involved.

(i) You must understand the working of the various types of internal funds, in particular: repairs and renewals funds, reserve funds, consolidated loans fund, pension funds, insurance funds, and trust funds.

(j) Revise the legal requirements for local authorities to require insurance.

(k) Revise the elements of risk management.

(l) Be able to describe the various types of insurance.

(m) Revise how a public authority invests its funds, and be aware of its provisions of the Trustee Investments Act 1961.

(n) Be aware of the definition of financial control and how it operates in practice in the public sector.

(o) Revise how a public authority utilises competitive tenders or competitive quotations.

(p) Long–term contracts are an important part of public sector purchasing and you must be aware of the types of contract that a public authority may enter into. Be aware of the manner in which a public authority appraises the contracts, and controls the performance of the contract.

(q) Stocks again form an important area of public sector control and you must be aware of the manner in which a public authority will control its stocks.

4   **Financial procedures**

This area of the syllabus covers the financial procedures that govern, in the main, the movements of cash within a public authority.

(a) Make sure that you understand and can reproduce the procedures necessary for the following:

    (i) payment of wages and salaries;

    (ii) payment of creditors;

    (iii) payments and receipts out of petty cash;

    (iv) receipts of cash from debtors;

(v) receipts of cash income and the problems associated with movements of cash in general.

(b) Be aware of the main services that the clearing banks will offer to local authorities.

(c) Understand how local authorities use common, central services, and how the costs of these services may be allocated between different authorities.

(d) Consider the impact computing has made on the processes of financial management, especially with reference to management information systems and the growth of terminal input and retrieval.

INDEX TO QUESTIONS AND ANSWERS

QUESTIONS

1 THE ORGANISATION

1.1 PASSAGE OF DIRECTIVES

(a) Explain how central government passes directives and information to public
sector organisations. (15 marks)

(b) Quote and describe one recent example of legislation affecting a public
sector organisation. (10 marks)

1.2 TWO–TIER STRUCTURE (J86)

The administrative pattern of many public sector organisations is based on a two
tier structure.

Required

(a) Define what you understand by a two tier structure, illustrating the
respective functions of the tiers by reference to a public sector organisation
of your choice. (10 marks)

(b) Outline the advantages and disadvantages generally associated with a two
tier structure from the respective viewpoints of both the public **and** the
officers of the organisation. (15 marks)

1.3 FUNCTIONAL v SERVICE BASIS (D87)

Finance departments are frequently organised on either a functional or a service
basis.

Required

(a) Distinguish between these two alternative forms of organisation. (5 marks)

(b)   Outline the advantages and disadvantages of both a functional and a service organisation.   (10 marks)

(c)   Outline the essential requirements of a successful organisation structure.
                                                                          (10 marks)

1.4   GOVERNMENT CONTROL (D88)

(a)   Outline **four** principal reasons why central government exerts control over many of the services provided by public sector organisations.   (8 marks)

(b)   Illustrate your **four** reasons with examples from a public sector organisation of your choice.   (8 marks)

(c)   Many public corporations, eg, British Rail and the Post Office, are or have been converted into large industrial companies which puts them outside the direct control of central government. You are required to identify **three** key features which distinguish public corporations from large industrial companies.   (9 marks)

1.5   ADMINISTRATIVE STRUCTURE (J89)

(a)   Describe the administrative structure of **either** the National Health Service **or** local government.   (13 marks)

(b)   Indicate the main functions of the various administrative tiers described in your answer to (a).   (12 marks)

Students should identify which country they are referring to in their answer.

1.6   PRIVATISATION (D89)

Since the General Election in 1979, the organisation and structure of the public sector has been significantly altered.

(a)   Describe **four** policy aims of the privatisation strategy pursued by the government; illustrate with appropriate examples.   (12 marks)

(b)   Identify **four** advantages which are claimed might result from the policy to allow certain public sector institutions to opt out of public sector control and become self–governing bodies. Illustrate your answer with appropriate examples.   (8 marks)

(c)   Explain **two** problems which are claimed might be created for organisations remaining in the main stream of the public sector, as a result of implementing the policies outlined in either (a) or (b) above.   (5 marks)

1.7   NATURE, ENVIRONMENT AND FUNCTIONS (J90)

Outline the ways in which the distinctive nature, environment and functions of public sector organisations place limits on their organisation and operation.

Illustrate your answer with relevant examples.

1.8   GOVERNMENTAL ROLES (D91)

(a)   Using a central government department of your choice describe the main functions of a minister or Secretary of State.   (10 marks)

(b)   Explain with examples the role of Parliamentary Select Committees.

(7 marks)

(c)   Describe the status and role of the National Audit Office and the Audit Commission for Local Authorities and the National Health Service in England and Wales.   (8 marks)

1.9   PUBLIC SECTOR FINANCE (D91)

(a)   Construct a diagram outlining the organisational structure of a typical finance department (you are not required to provide details of post titles, staff numbers and grades). Clearly identify the principal functions of the key sections.   (7 marks)

(b)   Describe both the general structure (with a brief example) and purpose of a coding system to analyse income and expenditure in a public sector organisation.   (12 marks)

(c)   Identify **six** items of information to be included on the record of fixed assets for a public sector organisation.   (6 marks)

2   MANAGEMENT – POLICY AND STRUCTURE

2.1   FINANCE COMMITTEE

(a)   Describe the purpose, composition and functions of a committee responsible for finance in a public sector organisation;   (15 marks)

(b)   List the duties of its chairman; and   (5 marks)

(c)   Compare the role of members to that of officers.   (5 marks)

2.2   CORPORATE MANAGEMENT

(a)   Explain the concept of corporate management.   (13 marks)

(b)   Describe the strengths and weaknesses of corporate management in a public sector organisation.   (12 marks)

2.3   ROLE OF OFFICERS (D86)

Describe the respective roles of officers and elected or appointed members in managing the finances of a public sector organisation.   (15 marks)

Explain the administrative arrangements that public sector organisations make to facilitate the carrying out of these roles.   (10 marks)

2.4   POLICY MAKING (D86)

Policy making in the public sector is frequently made by an incremental approach which accepts the existing level of service and plans only for small changes from year to year.

(a)   Identify the strengths and weaknesses of the incremental approach to policy making.   (12 marks)

(b)   Describe the main stages of the **rational or logical approach** to policy making which is frequently put forward as an alternative method of deciding policies for public sector organisations. (13 marks)

2.5   COMMUNICATION (J87)

Effective communication is essential to the work of an accounting technician. You are required to briefly define communication and outline:

(a)   the factors which contribute to an effective communication process; (5 marks)

(b)   the reasons why the communication process in an organisation frequently breaks down. (5 marks)

(c)   Write notes on **three different** methods or means of communication which an accounting technician could make use of in the public sector. (15 marks)

2.6   THE THREE Es (J87)

(a)   Compare and contrast the meaning of the terms economy, efficiency and effectiveness in a public sector environment. Illustrate your answer with appropriate examples from one or more parts of the public sector. (12 marks)

(b)   Discuss the strengths and weaknesses of using unit costs to measure the performance of public sector organisations. (13 marks)

2.7   FIVE TERMS (J88)

Explain **three** of the following management terms in the context of a public sector organisation:

(a)   span of control;
(b)   corporate management;
(c)   delegation;
(d)   internal check;
(e)   employee appraisal.

2.8   ZBB/CLF (D89)

Describe the operation and list **four** benefits of **both** of the following:

(a)   zero–based budgeting (ZBB);
(b)   consolidated loans fund (CLF).

2.9   PLANNING, DIRECTING, ORGANISING AND CONTROLLING (J90)

Planning, directing, organising and controlling are frequently identified as the four major activities of effective management.

(a)   Explain, with examples from a public sector organisation of your choice, each of these four major activities. (18 marks)

(b)   Distinguish between the terms **authority** and **responsibility**, then illustrate your explanation by reference to the work of an accounting technician. (7 marks)

2.10 INTERVIEWS (J91)

A vacancy has arisen in your section for an accountancy assistant who must be a qualified accounting technician. You are to play a major role in making this appointment and obviously wish to perform the task well. You will chair the interview panel consisting of a representative of the personnel department and another section had in the finance department. To assist you in conducting the interviews, you decide to undertake some preparatory work.

Required

(a)   Describe **five** items of information to be found in the job description for the accountancy assistant which might be of use to you at the interview.

(5 marks)

(b)   Draw up a brief plan explaining how you will structure and conduct the interview.   (8 marks)

(c)   Design an interview record form which would allow you to assess the interviewees' performance against **six** key assessment criteria. You should provide accompanying notes which expand the assessment criteria, for example in terms of what is being assessed and/or the subject matter and purpose of questions which might be asked at the interview. The answer should be in a form which is usable at the interview.   (12 marks)

3   FINANCIAL CONTROL AND MANAGEMENT

3.1   WORKING BALANCE

(a)   What is the purpose of a working balance?   (5 marks)

(b)   Suggest areas of expenditure and income of a public sector organisation that may affect the size of working balance.   (20 marks)

3.2   CONTROL OF PAYMENT

(a)   Briefly state why financial control over the ordering of and payment for goods and services is necessary and explain how this may be exercised.

(19 marks)

(b)   Briefly describe:

(i)   virement   (2 marks)
(ii)   contingency   (2 marks)
(iii)   financial commitment   (2 marks)

3.3   INCREASING COSTS

(a)   Give reasons why rents, fees and charges are generally increasing in a specified public sector organisation.   (10 marks)

(b)   Suggest factors that should be considered in renewing and calculating increases within one specified service.   (15 marks)

3.4 STOCK OF GOODS

'The stock of goods held by a public sector organisation is a valuable asset.'

(a) Describe the principal controls that management should consider relating to stock. (17 marks)

(b) List the typical procedures for ordering, receipt and issue of a stores item, mentioning the documents used. (8 marks)

3.5 VARIOUS ROLES

Describe the role of:

(a) chief financial officer; (6 marks)
(b) qualified accountant; (6 marks)
(c) qualified accountant technician; (6 marks)

within a public sector organisation.

Show the working relationship between each of the above. (7 marks)

3.6 LEISURE CENTRE

Identify and examine the factors which need to be considered when reviewing the charges for a leisure centre.

3.7 BUDGET PREPARATION

(a) Describe the process of budget preparation in a public sector organisation. (20 marks)

(b) Describe the role of the Chief Financial Officer in financial control. (5 marks)

3.8 WORKING GROUP

(a) What is the purpose of a multi-disciplinary working group of senior officers? (15 marks)

(b) Outline the role of a finance officer in serving with such a group. (10 marks)

3.9 CONTRACT TENDER

(a) Explain the procedures of a public sector organisation in seeking, assessing and accepting a tender for a capital contract. (20 marks)

(b) Describe the Chief Financial Officer's role relating to contract payments. (5 marks)

3.10 COST-BENEFIT ANALYSIS

(a) What do you understand by the term 'cost benefit analysis'? (15 marks)

(b) In what ways is cost-benefit analysis useful for a public sector organisation? (10 marks)

3.11 EXPENDITURE

Define:

(a)	capital expenditure;	(4 marks)
(b)	revenue expenditure;	(5 marks)

and give two examples which illustrate and contrast.

(c) Select one public sector organisation and explain how its revenue expenditure is financed indicating any recent changes or trends. (16 marks)

3.12 DIRECT CHARGING

(a) Direct charging for services is becoming an increasing source of finance to many public authorities. How do you account for this change? (5 marks)

(b) What factors should public authorities take into consideration when fixing charges for services? (20 marks)

Note: Your answer should make reference to a public authority with which you are familiar.

3.13 PROJECT FACTORS

Outline, with reasons, the main financial and non-financial factors you would include in a comprehensive report to a committee, which is to consider whether a project should be included in a public authority's capital expenditure programme.

3.14 RISK AND REPERCUSSIONS (J86)

The repercussions for a public sector organisation if a contractor goes into liquidation whilst carrying out a capital contract are numerous. You are required to describe and evaluate the effectiveness of two methods of reducing the risk and repercussions of such an occurrence, namely:

(a)	financial vetting of contractors prior to awarding a contract;	(15 marks)
(b)	performance bonding.	(10 marks)

3.15 OFFICIAL ORDER FORMS (J86)

(a) Outline **three** ways in which the use of official order forms can assist financial control. (9 marks)

(b) Describe the principal checks that should be carried out on an invoice for goods received before a cheque is despatched to the supplier. Indicate, giving your reasons, which officers should carry out each check. (16 marks)

3.16 MANPOWER BUDGET (J86)

Your organisation is considering preparing a manpower budget and the chief financial officer has been asked to supply information on the topic. As an accounting technician located in the research and information section of the finance department you have been asked to gather the information.

Required

(a)   Summarise the steps involved in preparing a manpower budget.   (8 marks)

(b)   Outline the likely advantages that might accrue to the organisation from preparing a manpower budget.   (9 marks)

(c)   Indicate any problems that might be encountered in preparing a manpower budget.   (8 marks)

3.17   SOURCE OF FUNDING (D86)

You are an accounting technician located in the finance department of a public sector organisation of your choice. Your section head has asked you to prepare a document which explains clearly the organisation's source of funding and how those funds are expended.

(a)   Prepare the explanatory document requested by your section head.

(17 marks)

(b)   Identify **two** interested groups who might make use of such a document. What benefits might the groups gain from using such a document?

(8 marks)

3.18   TENDERING (D86)

(a)   Describe and distinguish between:

(i)   open tendering **and** selective tendering;
(ii)   fixed price tenders **and** fluctuating price tenders.   (8 marks)

(b)   Outline **five** checks that should be made by the chief financial officer prior to paying interim certificates on a long–term capital contract.

(5 marks)

(c)   Identify the key points to be included in a set of financial rules governing the procedures for the letting of contracts for routine goods and services. Candidates should concentrate on procedures between the time it is decided to go out to tender and actually signing the tender document.   (12 marks)

3.19   INTERNAL FUNDS (D86)

Public sector organisations frequently establish internal funds for a variety of purposes.

(a)   Describe the purpose and operation of **two** internal funds of your choice. You should state clearly the type of public sector organisation where such funds are to be found.   (12 marks)

(b)   Discuss the principal tasks involved in the financial management of internal funds.   (13 marks)

3.20   MONITORING (J87)

As an accounting technician in the finance department of a public sector organisation your primary responsibility is the monitoring of revenue expenditure of a particular service department. In the near future you are going to discuss budgetary control procedures with your opposite number in the service department.

In order to prepare for the meeting you are required to:

(a)   briefly describe budgetary control;   (5 marks)

(b)   outline the layout and headings that might be appropriate for a monthly budget statement, produced by the finance department, in order to allow a budget holder in the service department to monitor revenue expenditure. Explain the reasons why you have selected such a format;   (12 marks)

(c)   distinguish between income and expenditure accounting and commitment accounting.   (8 marks)

3.21   EXPLAIN TERMS (D87)

Explain, in the context of a public authority budgeting system, the following terms:

(a)   contingency provision;
(b)   working balance
(c)   financing capital expenditure from revenue;
(d)   supplementary estimates.

3.22   CODING (D87)

Coding structures are the cornerstone of budgetary control systems in public sector organisations.

(a)   Outline the essential characteristics of an effective coding structure.

(6 marks)

(b)   Describe and illustrate with an example, the coding structure for revenue expenditure operated by a public sector organisation of your choice.

(12 marks)

(c)   Outline the benefits which can accrue from using a coding structure for controlling the stock of materials in a public sector transport depot.

(7 marks)

3.23   NEW SOURCES OF INCOME (J88)

Public sector organisations are increasingly looking for new sources of income to fund expenditure. Thus many establishments such as hospitals, schools, etc, are undertaking private fund raising to finance school trips, hospital libraries, etc.

(a)   Draft a set of guidelines which would ensure such funds are properly utilised and controlled.   (18 marks)

(b)   Describe briefly the principal features of a system to ensure sundry debtors accounts are collected in a cost effective manner.   (7 marks)

3.24   FINANCIAL CONTROL (J88)

(a)   What do you understand by the term 'financial control'?   (6 marks)

(b)   Identify **five** features which are essential to the development of effective financial control systems in public sector organisations.   (10 marks)

(c) Describe **one** example of external financial controls which influence each of the following types of public sector organisations:

    (i)   the National Health Service;
    (ii)   local authorities.   (9 marks)

Students in answer to (c) above should provide a **different** example for each type of public sector organisation.

3.25   REVENUE BUDGETS (J88)

(a) Outline **five** reasons why revenue budgets are prepared by public sector organisations.   (10 marks)

(b) Describe the procedures and processes through which a public sector organisation of your choice prepares the approves its annual revenue budget.   (15 marks)

3.26   FUNDED v UNFUNDED (J88)

(a) Providing an example of each, distinguish between a funded and an unfunded superannuation scheme.   (6 marks)

(b) Briefly describe **three** types of income and **three** types of expenditure one might expect to find in a funded superannuation scheme.   (6 marks)

(c) Explain with examples the **three** main categories of investment as defined by the Trustee Investment Act 1961.   (10 marks)

(d) Explain briefly the role of an actuary in relation to a superannuation fund.   (3 marks)

3.27   PUBLIC SECTOR CHARGES (D88)

(a) Giving an example of each explain the distinction between the following categories of public sector charges:

    (i)   nominal;
    (ii)   statutory;
    (iii)   means tested.   (9 marks)

(b) Explain the operation of a successful assessment scale.   (6 marks)

(c) Outline **five** essential characteristics of a successful assessment scale.   (10 marks)

3.28   PUBLIC SECTOR ACCOUNTANTS (D88)

Public sector accountants are frequently being located in service departments, eg, unit accountants in the National Health Service, and also in finance sections of polytechnics and other local authority departments.

Required

(a) Define the role and functions of such an accountant.   (13 marks)

(b) Explain with reasons the possible management arrangements for such a post.   (12 marks)

3.29 BUDGETARY FLEXIBILITY (D88)

Your section head has recently received a memorandum from a budget holder in a department of your organisation. The budget holder explains that he/she is becoming increasingly frustrated at not being able to manage their budget in a flexible way. The budget holder writes that it would motivate budget holders if they were given freedom to spend within a fixed revenue budget allocation.

Required

(a) Outline **four** problems of allowing budget holders to spend freely within a given fixed budget allocation. (13 marks)

(b) Describe **four** ways in which budget holders can be given flexibility in the management of their budgets. Illustrate your answer with appropriate examples. (12 marks)

3.30 INVESTMENT APPRAISAL (D88)

A public sector organisation is considering investing in two alternative investments. The projects are as follows:

		£'000	£'000
Initial capital cost		150	250
Annual net income			
Year	1	50	25
	2	50	25
	3	50	25
	4	37.5	25
	5		50
	6		100
	7		125
	8		150
Life of project		4 years	8 years

Required

(a) Compare the two capital projects using the payback period and the average annual rate of return on average capital employed. (8 marks)

(b) Outline the respective advantages of the two investment appraisal methods employed in (a) above. (9 marks)

(c) Explain what you understand by the term **discounted cashflow** in relation to investment appraisal. Illustrate your answer by reference to the data in (a) above. (Note, calculations are **not** required in answer to this part of the question.) (8 marks)

3.31 FIVE PRINCIPLES (J89)

(a) Describe **five** principles which, in your opinion, should form the basis of any central government grants to public sector organisations. (15 marks)

(b) Explain the following terms:

(i) external financing limits;
(ii) grant-related expenditure assessment;
(iii) public expenditure survey system. (10 marks)

3.32   FINANCE DEPARTMENT (J89)

(a)   Providing an example of each describe **six** major functions performed by a finance department of a public sector organisation of your choice. (18 marks)

(b)   Giving a reason, outline **three** areas of work which a chief financial officer is unlikely to delegate on a regular basis to one of his/her staff.   (7 marks)

3.33   INTERNAL AUDIT (J89)

(a)   Identify **five** points which are likely to be included in financial regulations governing the operation of internal audit.   (15 marks)

(b)   Define and contrast the meaning of the terms internal audit and internal check in a public sector environment.

Illustrate your answer with appropriate examples.   (10 marks)

3.34   FINANCING EXPENDITURE (J89)

Discuss **four** advantages and **four** disadvantages for **each** of the following methods of financing expenditure in public sector organisations:

(a)   leasing;
(b)   temporary borrowing.

3.35   PAY (D89)

(a)   Identify **three** possible benefits for employers moving from weekly to monthly pay for manual workers.   (6 marks)

(b)   Describe the possible ways of overcoming problems of introducing monthly payment for weekly–paid staff.   (9 marks)

(c)   Describe **five** possible benefits you would use to convince employees in your organisation to open a bank account and have their wages paid into the account.   (10 marks)

3.36   OBJECTIVES (D89)

(a)   Identify **four** reasons why the setting of objectives is so essential to the planning process of public sector organisations.   (12 marks)

(b)   Describe **three** key objectives which are likely to be set for internal audit in a public sector organisation.   (9 marks)

(c)   Outline, briefly, the role of a chief financial officer in formulating the objectives of a public sector organisation.   (4 marks)

3.37   CAPITAL PROGRAMMES AND BUDGETS (J90)

(a)   Describe **four** reasons why public sector organisations prepare capital programmes and budgets.   (8 marks)

(b)   Describe **four** items of financial information which should be available to decision–makers considering the merits of a proposed capital project. Explain why you have selected these **four** items.   (8 marks)

(c)   Giving examples of each, explain the following terms used in relation to capital projects:

    (i)   variation orders;
    (ii) provisional sums;
    (iii) interim certificates.   (9 marks)

3.38   INSURANCE TERMS AND INSURANCE FUNDS (J90)

(a)   Explain the following insurance terms:

    (i)   employer's liability insurance;
    (ii) fidelity guarantee insurance;
    (iii) doctrine of uberrimae fidei;
    (iv) average clause.   (16 marks)

(b)   Describe the operation and purpose of an insurance fund in a public sector organisation.   (5 marks)

(c)   Outline **two** advantages and **two** disadvantages which might result from setting up an insurance fund.   (4 marks)

3.39   STAFFING LEVELS AND BONUS SCHEMES (J90)

The largest proportion of revenue expenditure of most public sector organisations is incurred on employees.

(a)   Describe **three** ways in which public sector bodies may reduce staffing levels, outlining the advantages and disadvantages of each approach.

                                   (19 marks)

(b)   List **three** benefits and **three** drawbacks which might accrue to a public sector organisation if it paid some employees via a bonus scheme.   (6 marks)

3.40   RECENT LEGISLATION (J91)

(a)   The Local Government and Housing Act 1989 introduced major changes to several parts of local government finance.

    Write notes on each of the following points of the Act:

    (i)   discretionary expenditure, describing briefly the position before and after the 1989 Act;   (5 marks)

    (ii) definition of capital expenditure;   (5 marks)

    (iii) borrowing and borrowing limits.   (8 marks)

(b)   As a result of the White Paper 'Working for patients', the National Health Service is introducing capital charges into its budgets.

    Explain both the method of calculating the charges and **three** objectives of introducing capital charges.   (7 marks)

3.41   TAXALL DISTRICT COUNCIL (J91)

You are employed as an accounting technician in the Community Charge section of Taxall District Council. The following letter has been received from Mrs A Grant, a community charge payer of the District.

Questions

'Dear Sir,

In previous years, I have left it to my husband to pay the rates but last year I received a bill from your authority for £356.80 in respect of the 19X0/X1 community charge. The bill I am informed is arrived at in the following way.

		£ per head of population
Bakershire County Council Precept		777.00
Taxall District Council		88.50
Thatcham Parish Council		1.40
Total demand on collection fund		866.90
Deduct: Business rate	292.51	
Revenue support grant	217.59	
		510.10
		356.80

'Nobody enjoys paying taxes but I feel more could have been done to explain the tax. As ever, the jargon of accountants makes it difficult to understand what I am paying for. I would be grateful if you could explain in plain English what the above figures and terminology mean. Words like precept, collection fund, business rate, revenue support grant, etc, are confusing.

'Finally somewhere on my bill there is a figure of £278.00 which is described as the SSA level. I don't know what this is. Am I correct in thinking that I have been charged £78.80 too much and this will be deducted from my 19X1/X2 bill?'

Required

Draft a letter responding to Mrs Grant's complaints. The content of your letter will be approved by your section head who has stressed that the tone of the letter should be 'positive and professional'.

3.42   DEVHAM COUNTY (D91)

The directors of leisure and recreation of the District Councils in the Devham County area have produced the following statistics in respect of 19X0/X1 net expenditure per head of population for leisure and recreation at county level (ie, both tiers of the shire authority are combined).

	Devham County area £	Average of 40 county areas £
Recreation – Indoor	2.73	6.74
– Outdoor	4.37	6.99
Arts promotion and facilities	0.81	3.90
Tourism	0.68	1.07
Catering	(0.06)	(0.07)
Administration and other	1.13	2.33
Total	9.66	20.96

The directors have commented that the statistics reveal Devham to be below the average expenditure levels and in fact the county area is the 32nd lowest spender of the 40 county areas. The leisure directors have informed the directors of finance that they feel the statistics will support their claims for increased budget provisions in future years.

As an accounting technician you are asked to prepare a memorandum to the directors of finance to attempt the following.

(a) Evaluate the significance of the above statistics highlighting any calculations or additional information you feel are relevant.   (12 marks)

(b) Suggest an alternative method of comparing the financial performance of the leisure and recreation function with other authorities.   (4 marks)

(c) Explain how and why public sector organisations should distinguish between efficiency and effectiveness in the provision of services. Illustrate your answer with examples.   (9 marks)

3.43   BUDGETARY CONTROL (D91)

Your organisation is delegating responsibility for the preparation and management of service budgets to middle managers in service departments. You are discussing this change with a colleague who will be given responsibility for a budget in the near future. Your colleague comments that the thought of managing a budget fills him/her with fear and apprehension as his/her background is non–financial. The colleague is very doubtful about what effective budgetary control involves.

Respond to your colleague, informing him/her of the following.

(a) The objectives of the proposed change to the budget process.   (6 marks)

(b) The reasons why your colleague's fears might be justified.   (9 marks)

(c) Ways in which such fears may be reduced and achieve effective budgetary control.   (10 marks)

3.44   BUDGET STATEMENT (D91)

The following is an extract from a budget statement for the catering department in a public sector organisation; the statement covers the nine months to December 19X1.

	Annual budget £	Budget for period £	Expenditure for period £	Variance £
Salaries and wages	146,236	109,677	107,632	2,045
Provisions	65,455	49,092	53,815	4,723

(a) Comment on the format of the statement indicating, with reasons, **four** additions you would make to the statement in order to improve its usefulness to budget holders.   (8 marks)

(b) Identify **six** possible reasons for each of the variances.   (4 marks)

(c)   Distinguish between the terms virement and a supplementary estimate, indicating how financial control might be exercised over their application.

(8 marks)

(d)   Comment on the following information: the budget for a period was set at £20,000 to produce 15,000 x-rays whereas in the period the department produced 1,200 x-rays at a total cost of £18,000.   (5 marks)

3.45   CAPITAL EXPENDITURE (D91)

(a)   Identify **six** factors to be considered when a public sector organisation is deciding how to finance capital expenditure.   (12 marks)

(b)   Describe **six** reasons why public sector organisations prepare capital budgets.   (9 marks)

(c)   Explain briefly what you understand by cost benefit analysis.   (4 marks)

4   FINANCIAL PROCEDURES

4.1   PETTY CASH

(a)   What is the purpose of petty cash?   (5 marks)

(b)   Describe a procedure, with controls necessary, for operating a petty cash account.   (20 marks)

4.2   CASHFLOW

(a)   What is meant by cashflow?   (10 marks)

(b)   Comment on its importance to a public sector organisation and suggest ways in which it could be improved.   (15 marks)

4.3   CLEARING BANK SERVICES

(a)   Describe the following services which a public sector organisation might receive from a clearing bank:

    (i)   operation of a current account;
    (ii)   overdraft facility;
    (iii) payment of salaries and wages;
    (iv) supply of computer magnetic tapes;
    (v)   direct bank to bank transfer payments.   (16 marks)

(b)   State the procedures required in reconciling a bank balance with a cash book balance. Give a simple numeric example.   (9 marks)

4.4   ALLOCATION OF COSTS

(a)   Describe central administrative expenses and the **reasons** for allocation.

(15 marks)

(b)   Describe **methods** which may be used for allocating these costs.   (10 marks)

4.5 **CHANGING BANKERS**

(a) Your authority is considering changing its bankers. Outline how such a change could be achieved and the problems which might be encountered.

(13 marks)

(b) Outline the methods of charging for facilities which are employed by the banks. (12 marks)

4.6 **CHECKING INVOICES**

Invoices should be checked by a public authority both before and after they are paid. Describe the system by which these checks should be made.

4.7 **CENTRAL STORES (D86)**

Draft a set of financial instructions to be followed in respect of the following aspects of central stores procedure and control:

(a) receipt of goods;
(b) issue of goods;
(c) stock levels.

4.8 **BLAKESHIRE REGIONAL HEALTH AUTHORITY (J87)**

J Smith has recently been appointed general manager of Blakeshire Regional Health Authority; Smith was previously employed as a marketing director of a national food retailer. One of the first suggestions Smith makes when taking up his appointment is that district health authorities should consider setting up a central purchasing and storage facility for common use items, such as office stationery, medical supplies and equipment, cleaning materials, etc. Smith's suggestion is to be discussed at the July meeting of district finance officers.

As an accounting technician employed in the finance department of one of the district health authorities you are required to prepare a report to the district finance officer outlining:

(a) the general considerations to be borne in mind when evaluating any proposal to establish joint-use facilities;

(b) the issues, financial and other, that would need to be included in any contract between the district health authorities.

4.9 **CASHFLOW MANAGEMENT (J87)**

(a) What do you understand by the term 'cashflow management'? In what ways will effective cashflow management benefit a public authority?

(10 marks)

(b) As cash transactions gradually diminish the debtors of public authorities are settling their debts in various ways. You are required to outline the advantages and disadvantages to public authorities of the following methods of payment:

(i) cheque;
(ii) direct debit;
(iii) standing orders;
(iv) credit cards. (15 marks)

4.10 REGULATIONS (D87)

(a) List **ten** principal procedures that are usually covered by the financial regulations, instructions or their equivalent in a public sector organisation of your choice. Candidates should not use the examples quoted in part (b) of this question. (5 marks)

(b) Write a typical set of instructions to cover **two** of the following procedures:

    (i)   payments for goods and services;
    (ii)   trust funds;
    (iii) inventories. (20 marks)

4.11 PAYROLL (D88)

Draft a list of financial regulations/instructions covering the payment of employees in a public sector organisation. The regulations should cover the engagement of employees, the preparation of payroll and the payment of wages in cash.

4.12 IMPREST (D89)

(a) Explain the operation and purpose of a petty cash imprest in a public sector organisation. (9 marks)

(b) Write a typical set of financial regulations covering the procedures for operating and controlling an imprest account. (16 marks)

4.13 CENTRALISED SERVICES (J90)

(a) Identify **six** financial services which are likely to be administered centrally in a public sector organisation. (3 marks)

(b) Describe **three** major benefits which might result from centralisation of the services identified in (a) above.

Illustrate **each** benefit with a relevant example. (9 marks)

(c) What basis of recharge would you suggest for reallocating the cost of the following central services:

    (i)   central administrative buildings;
    (ii)   architectural services;
    (iii) personnel department;
    (iv) printing and reprographic services? (4 marks)

(d) Outline **three** key reasons for re–allocating the costs of central services to user departments. (9 marks)

4.14 BANK RECONCILIATION STATEMENTS (J91)

You are an accounting technician employed in the finance department of a polytechnic which has recently become responsible for managing its own finances. One of the department's tasks will be to prepare a monthly bank reconciliation statement. The polytechnic finance officer asks you to prepare a financial procedure document to assist staff in preparing bank reconciliations.

Required

Prepare such a document which should contain:

(a)   the basic procedures to be followed in constructing a bank reconciliation statement – the procedures should be in chronological order and clearly explained;   (15 marks)

(b)   a pro forma statement which could be used to explain why the balance on the bank statement is different from the balance on the cash book – the statement should be both comprehensive and clear in its content.

(10 marks)

Note: Candidates should produce a document which could be used in the finance department, not just a series of general points. Marks will be awarded for both the content and the presentation of the document.

4.15   PERSONAL COMPUTERS (J91)

Personal computers are widely used to process financial transactions and to assist managers in decision–making.

Required

(a)   Describe **eight** items of information likely to be recorded on an employee file in a computer payroll system.

(**Note:** Candidates should not refer to personnel records such as home address, holiday entitlements, etc).   (8 marks)

(b)   Define the term 'computerised financial model'. Illustrate your definition by reference to **three** models which could be constructed and used by an accounting technician in the public sector.   (7 marks)

(c)   List **five** advantages of using computerised financial modelling in the construction and management of a revenue budget in the public sector. Illustrate each advantage with an appropriate example.

(**Note:** Candidates should not use the same examples as used in answer to part (b) of this question.)   (10 marks)

4.16   WORKING CAPITAL (J91)

Discuss what you understand by the management of working capital in a public sector context. In what ways will the effective management of working capital benefit a public sector body? Illustrate your answer with relevant examples from the public sector.

5   CASE STUDIES

5.1   BRAMLEY

Bramley District Council has a department which is responsible for the collection and disposal of all household waste from the premises in the area. The productivity of this department has been compared unfavourably with that of outside contractors, and the council is under pressure to reduce its expenditure. It is the council's policy to keep as many of its services as possible under its own control.

Required

List, and explain briefly, all the factors which should be reviewed to improve the department's performance.

5.2 INDUCTION PROGRAMME

The team of which you have been a leader for the last two years has been engaged since that date on a systems development project which will take a further two years to complete. The six team members are drawn from a variety of disciplines and have different skill levels. Some are single, some married, with or without children, and one has recently been divorced. The team has been working very effectively. You have just been promoted, and have been asked to induct the new team leader, John Newby, who has been working for the organisation for some years.

Required

Prepare a list of **ten** items which you will include in your induction programme and explain why you include each one.

5.3 LOCAL AUTHORITY

One of the activities of a local authority is headed by a manager responsible for approximately 40 professionally–qualified staff, plus ancillary workers. Section heads look after groups of between three and six staff. The previous manager had an abrasive personality; he closely observed the performance, weaknesses and strengths of each member of staff, commented on them, and was unpopular with them and his superiors. The activities were efficient and highly regarded. Staff used to take part in many discretionary activities such as involvement with the public, and voluntary unpaid overtime.

A year ago a new manager, business school trained, was appointed. He promoted two section heads to be assistant managers, one for contact with the public, the other for administration, responsible for a new system of weekly performance reports and briefing meetings.

25% of the staff have left and the rest have gradually ceased all their discretionary activities. There is now a policy of positive non–cooperation.

Required

Analyse the situation, explain it on the basis of theory and suggest **four** reasons why it might have arisen.

5.4 CHARLES

Charles is in his early thirties and has been working in a large government office since he left school. He enjoys working with his colleagues and has progressed steadily to his own and the organisation's satisfaction. He has made many friends at work, and is a member of his department's darts team. This requires him to practise frequently with the team at a local meeting place. One evening a week he goes with his wife to the dramatic society of which he is a member.

He has two children and two years ago took out a substantial loan to move to a larger house. Rising interest rates are now making the family budgeting more difficult.

A vacancy within the same government department has been publicised for which Charles is technically ideally qualified. It would mean a big rise in salary, making his financial position very satisfactory, plus a car. The job consists of regularly inspecting a large number of unmanned sites scattered around the country, reading gauges accurately, recording the information, and reporting it to his manager.

Required

Discuss how suitable this job is for Charles, both from his point of view and from that of the organisation, backing your discussion with relevant theory.

1   THE ORGANISATION

1.1   PASSAGE OF DIRECTIVES

(a)   Public sector organisations receive power by General Acts of Parliament, known as Enabling Acts. These Acts lay down basic principles and confer explicit powers on the designated sponsoring minister. Details are then usually specified and extended by statutory instruments drawn up by the Minister or Secretary of State and the civil servants.

A local authority receives power through a Local Act of Parliament (although this can be a prolonged and expensive process); if it then proves to contain wider benefits it may be enacted as a General Act.

The major role of a minister responsible for a public corporation is to relate corporation activities to wider social and economic considerations. This function is discharged by means of general directives. These directives are increasingly issued in the form of ministerial letters and circulars which contain instructions, information and general suggestions. Such circulars carry considerable weight and, in effect, must be obeyed.

(b)   The Social Security and Housing Benefits Act 1982 has affected the public sector organisations by provisions for statutory sick pay and housing benefits. English law has long recognised that where primary reliance is placed upon earning capacity as a source of a minimum income, loss of that capacity due to inability to work by reason of sickness should be covered by an efficient social security system.

The provisions for statutory sick pay have transferred the responsibility for paying the sick employee for the first eight weeks to the employer. The rates of these weekly payments are related to earnings. After the first eights weeks the employer's liability for sickness pay ceases and state sickness benefit is payable. The employer is reimbursed by deducting the sum of his sickness payments from his monthly remittance for National Insurance contributions.

Directives contained in the Social Security Act 1986 changed the rules with effect from 1 April 1988.

(i)   Housing Benefit (HB) assessment has been brought into line with that for National Income support.

(ii)   HB is therefore assessed on net income, not gross as before April 1988.

(iii)   Each case has to be assessed by local authorities; there are no certificated HB cases.

(iv)   The maximum level of assistance for rent remains at 100%, although that for rates/community charge has been restricted to 80%.

(v)   No HB is available on water charges.

    (vi)   Claimants with capital exceeding £8,000 are not entitled to HB.

    (vii)   There are now two types: one for rents and one for the community charge.

1.2   TWO–TIER STRUCTURE

(a)   The administrative pattern referred to in the question refers to the structure within which the various functions carried out by public sector organisations operate. This pattern is laid down by legislation passed by Parliament. The majority of public sector functions are divided over the various administrative tiers. For example, in the water industry there are Regional Water Authorities and divisions; in the National Health Service there are Regional Health Authorities and District Health Authorities and finally in local government there are county councils and district councils.

These are all examples of a two–tier structure where each tier of administration performs various functions for the general public. It could be argued that there are additional tiers over and above those referred to above, for example, central government greatly influences the administrative tiers via circulars, grants, etc; furthermore, in local government there are parish councils which might be seen as a fourth tier of government. The fact is however that whilst central government and parish councils are part of the administrative pattern they do not, in the main, provide services directly to the public. It is therefore quite reasonable to refer to the administrative pattern of public sector organisations as being two–tier in many instances. I will illustrate this point in the remaining part of this answer by reference to the structure of local government in England.

If we exclude London, the system of local government in England (until 1 April 1986) was based on the Local Government Act 1972. This Act put forward two styles of local government, namely:

(i)   the metropolitan; and
(ii)   the non–metropolitan.

In this setting the functions of local government were divided between two tiers of authorities:

(i)   the county councils; and
(ii)   the metropolitan and non–metropolitan district councils.

The functions of local government were divided between two tiers of authorities – the county councils and the district councils. These bodies are independent of each other, both financially and constitutionally; this means that whilst the tiers frequently cooperate to provide services there is no suggestion that the county council is administratively more important than the district council and vice versa. The fact is that the tiers provide different and often complementary functions. In the non–metropolitan areas the following are examples of the functions provided by the respective tiers.

County councils (eg Cheshire, Cornwall, Northumberland, Kent, etc)

–   Education
–   Fire service and public protection
–   Highways and transportation
–   Libraries and leisure
–   Planning and industrial development

- Police
- Social services

District councils (eg, Cotswold, Northampton, South Ribble, etc)

- Housing
- Environmental health
- Refuse collection
- Recreation and amenities
- Industrial development

In the six metropolitan areas up until 1 April 1986 the following were examples of the functions provided by the respective tiers.

Metropolitan county councils (eg, Greater Manchester, Merseyside, South Yorkshire, Tyne and Wear, West Midlands and West Yorkshire)

- Police and fire
- Highways and transportation
- Passenger transport
- Refuse disposal
- Consumer protection
- Structure plans

Metropolitan district councils (eg, Tameside, Liverpool, Sunderland, Birmingham, etc)

- Education
- Housing
- Environmental health
- Refuse collection
- Personal social services

The situation in the metropolitan areas changed from 1 April 1986 with the abolition of the metropolitan county councils. The changes meant that most of the functions previously exercised by the metropolitan county councils became the direct responsibility of the district councils. In some cases joint boards have been set up to run services such as police, fire and public transport. Joint boards are made up of elected councillors nominated by the district councils, and are accountable through them to their local electorates.

(b) The two-tier system has many advantages and disadvantages, which are in many ways common to both officers and the public. The possible advantages of the two-tier system include the following.

(i) The planning and administration of services can be provided at the most appropriate level, eg, services such as police and fire are perhaps more effective if planned and managed on a county-wide basis.

(ii) Economies of scale can accrue to the large county council, ie, they are cost-effective tiers of government, eg, central purchasing arrangements.

(iii) Local geographical and demographic features can be catered for in the level and scope of service provision, eg, provision of schools in rural areas.

0144V

(iv) The two-tier system offers more opportunity for authorities to be sensitive to local opinions and needs, eg, design and provision of council houses.

Overall the two-tier system attempts to provide a standard structure which allows officers to be sensitive to obvious differences between different areas of the country.

The disadvantages of a two-tier system include the following.

(i) The public can have difficulties in identifying which tier is responsible for providing which services. This confusion is perpetuated in local government as rates paid to district councils include a contribution for services provided by the county council.

(ii) Officers of both tiers spend a great deal of time setting up and servicing joint planning teams/committees comprising officers and members of county and district councils.

(iii) In local government, where there are elected representatives, much time can be spent ironing out political conflicts between the county council and district council.

(iv) The division of functions between the two tiers can lead to problems when planning and coordinating service provision. This is best illustrated by the refuse disposal function which is a county council responsibility whereas refuse collection is a responsibility of district councils.

(v) The abolition of the metropolitan county council was the result of the lack of a clear role of the metropolitan county council. This tier of local government had relatively few services to administer and frequently this led to conflict with district councils as the county tried to establish a role as, say, a strategic planning authority.

To conclude this answer it would be useful to point out that the above advantages and disadvantages are not found in every public authority. They will necessarily be prevalent in varying degrees as the two-tier system attempts to fulfil conflicting objectives. On the one hand public sector organisations can be more effective and sensitive to local needs when they are administered locally, eg, by a district council; but at the same time to provide an effective and economical service it is frequently necessary to employ a wider base, eg, a county council.

1.3 FUNCTIONAL v SERVICE BASIS

(a) The tasks performed by most finance departments can be classified in at least two ways; these are described as a service organisation and a functional organisation. The former would arrange the work of a finance department so that it corresponds to the services performed by the authority eg, an education section would provide all or most of the financial support services to schools, colleges etc.

Alternatively a functionally organised finance department would arrange the work according to the type of work undertaken irrespective of the service for whom the work is provided. Thus a functionally organised finance department would probably be divided into an audit section, a salaries and wages section, an income collection section, an accountancy section, a creditor payment section etc.

(b)   The finance department structured on a service basis has the following advantages and disadvantages.

Advantages

(i)   It allows better communications and working relationships to be established between the service department and finance department employees.

(ii)   Following on from (i) above such relationships allow the special requirements of individual departments to be catered for; this might involve amending a standard system to allow for service needs.

(iii)   Overall it encourages the development of expertise and skills of finance department employees in relation to a particular service.

Disadvantages

(i)   The encouragement of service specialisation can inhibit the development of a corporate approach to policy making and implementation. The needs of the service can supersede the needs of the organisation.

(ii)   There is a possibility that by concentrating all functions in one service section that fraud is easier to perpetrate. This is due to the reduction of the number of natural internal checks in the organisation structure. Staff performing different functions are located in one place and thus collusion in fraud becomes that little bit more possible.

The alternative functional organisation has advantages including:

(i)   the encouragement of specialisation in particular financial functions eg audit;

(ii)   the fostering of a corporate approach to policy making and service provision;

(iii)   the natural provision of internal check to minimise the possibility of fraud and error; this is because the recording and actioning of particular functions are carried out by different employees.

The disadvantages of such an approach are principally founded upon the fact that specialisation whilst providing benefits does mean it is difficult for management to implement change. For example employees might resist being moved between specialisms eg, audit to accounts and might also find it a bar to their career patterns.

(c)   The following is a list of the essential requirements of a successful structure:

(i)   Clearly defined objectives, policies and strategies for the organisation.

(ii)   Effective channels of communication both horizontally and vertically.

(iii)   Chains of command that are precisely defined and known to all employees.

(iv)   Officers have the authority to allow them to perform their responsibilities.

0144V

(v) Delegation which allows decisions to be taken at the most appropriate level in the organisation.

(vi) The introduction of systems and working practices which facilitate the achievement of objectives by members of staff.

(vii) Finally members of staff need to have their place in the organisation in terms of duties, responsibilities and authority, clearly defined and communicated to them say by means of a job description or job evaluation.

1.4 GOVERNMENT CONTROL

(a) Four reasons why central government exerts control over many services provided by public sector organisations.

(i) The central government needs to ensure that public sector organisations behave in a legal manner and that they do not incur illegal expenditure.

(ii) The government needs control and influence in order that national plans and strategies are implemented at a local level.

(iii) National standards for certain essential services are expected in our society; central government has a responsibility to ensure that minimum national standards of service are achieved locally.

(iv) Finally central government has a key role in managing the national economy; it is difficult to see how this role could be performed if central government did not monitor and, where necessary, control the expenditures of public sector organisations.

(b) The above reasons are now illustrated.

(i) The auditors of central government verify the legality of expenses incurred by such bodies as health authorities; this is usually achieved at the audit of an authority's final accounts.

(ii) Governments have national plans for such functions as the development of inner cities and the care of the elderly in the community. Both of these strategies need the cooperation and, where necessary, control of local authorities.

(iii) National standards are set by government, eg, norms for staffing ratios, unit costs for capital expenditure, length of housing waiting lists, etc. These standards can be used to coerce authorities to undertake particular schemes, etc.

(iv) The rate capping of local authorities and the system of cash limits are both examples of controls used to limit total public expenditure. This is seen as a key instrument of central government economic policy.

(c) Public corporations differ from large industrial companies in the following respects.

(i) A private company has a primary objective of making profits although there will be other objectives such as increasing market share, etc. This contrasts with a public corporation, which, while concerned with covering its costs and perhaps making a return on capital employed, will also provide services which satisfy social objectives and frequently do not generate a profit.

(ii)   The output of private companies is frequently a tangible product which can be assessed and measured as to quality and quantity. The public corporation frequently provides a service which is difficult to measure in terms of quality. This means that quality control is perhaps more difficult in the public corporation.

(iii)   The public corporations obtain their funds from three principal sources: from central government, from borrowing and from levying a charge for the provision of services. They do not, however, issue shares as does the public limited company. The company can declare dividends and create reserves, etc. Thus the capital structures of the two organisations are different.

1.5   ADMINISTRATIVE STRUCTURE

(a)   The present structure of the National Health Service (NHS) was established by the Health Services Act 1980 and became operative in 1982. This was further changed following the establishment of the Policy Board and Management Executive, and the recommendations in the 1989 White Paper, Working for Patients. In **England** the NHS is organised as a three tier administrative structure. Ultimately all tiers of the NHS are accountable to Parliament.

A summary of the structure in England and Wales is given below:

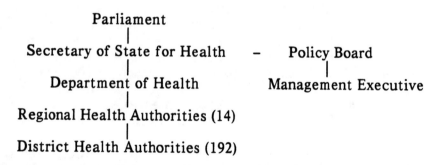

```
                    Parliament
                        |
     Secretary of State for Health    -    Policy Board
                        |                       |
            Department of Health         Management Executive
                        |
      Regional Health Authorities (14)
                        |
      District Health Authorities (192)
```

At the top of the NHS is the Secretary of State for Health, aided by the Minister for Health. These Ministers are served by the civil servants of the Department of Health.

The National Health Service Act 1977 sets out the powers and duties of the Secretary of State. The principal duties are to continue the promotion in England of a comprehensive health service designed to secure improvement

(i)   in the physical and mental health of the people of that country; and
(ii)   in the prevention, diagnosis and treatment of illness;

and for that purpose to provide or secure the effective provision of services in accordance with this Act.

The services so provided must be free except insofar as the making and recovery of charges is expressly provided for by or under any enactment, whenever passed.

0144V

It is the Secretary of State's duty to provide throughout England, to such extent as he considers necessary to meet all reasonable requirements:

(i)   hospital accommodation;

(ii)   medical, dental, nursing and ambulance services;

(iii)   facilities for the care of expectant and nursing mothers and young children as he considers are appropriate;

(iv)   facilities for the prevention of illness, the care of persons suffering from illness, and after-care of persons who have suffered from illness, as he considers appropriate;

(v)   other services as are required for the diagnosis and treatment of illness.

The key functions of the top tier, ie, the Secretary of State and the Department of Health, are centred on the duties outlined by the National Health Services Act 1977, as amended in 1989. This will entail establishing national plans, priorities and policies for the NHS and monitoring how successfully such policies are implemented by the lower tiers of the NHS. From 1989 a Policy Board comprising the Secretary of State and appointed members from industry was set up. It will determine the strategy, objectives and finances of the NHS in the light of government policy. It is to set objectives for the Management Executive which will have responsibility for the operation and management of the NHS within the framework set by ministers and the Policy Board. It is also responsible for setting health authorities' objectives, and monitoring them through the review processes. Having established plans and priorities it is the Secretary of State's responsibility to discuss with Cabinet colleagues priorities for an adequate share of the nation's resources to implement such plans. When the nation's expenditure plans have been agreed, the Secretary of State will be allocated a share of the national resources to administer the NHS. It is the Secretary of State's duty to distribute these resources throughout the country in order that the plans will be achieved. The Health Services Act 1980 made it mandatory for health authorities to keep their drawings within the approved cash limit plus any additional income which could be generated locally.

In England there are 14 Regional Health Authorities who interpret the policies established by the Department of Health. The regions cover geographical areas extending over several local authority boundaries. Regional Health Authorities are administered by persons appointed by the Secretary of State; the members will include doctors, a nurse or midwife, a representative of the region's medical school, and other representatives nominated by local authorities and trade unions.

Regional Health Authorities interpret the policies of the Department of Health and draw up policies in plans which suit their particular needs. This results in the preparation of regional strategic plans. These plans are produced after consultation with the third tier of the NHS, namely the District Health Authorities. The plans attempt to assess the health care pattern for particular regions over the following ten year period. The regional strategic plan must be submitted to the Department of Health for approval. When approved, the plans form the basis of health care policy over a period of time; obviously there is a need to review the operational aspects of such plans on an annual basis. Each Regional Health Authority is responsible for allocating the funds, received from the Department of Health, to the District Health Authorities within the region. These funds are allocated in a way which allows the regional strategic plan to be achieved. It is each region's responsibility to monitor the expenditure of its District Health Authorities.

Regions give advice to the districts on policy implementation and are directly responsible for managing some ambulance and blood transfusion services; also they will assist in designing and monitoring capital projects. Often the regions provide computer facilities for the districts so that the benefits of economies of scale may accrue.

There are 192 District Health Authorities (DHAs) in England. These authorities are responsible for providing hospital and community health services. Thus the DHAs are the providers of health services in line with policies set at a national and regional level. The districts attempt to apply policies set at the higher levels, while taking account of the nature and size of the local population. It is at the district level that health needs are identified and fed back into the planning systems of the Department of Health and the region. It is districts' responsibility to identify service deficiencies and to apply to the regions for funds to meet such deficiencies. More often than not, funds are not available and districts are forced either to cut existing services or find economies to fund the deficiencies. The funds allocated by the regions to DHAs are based on such indicators of need as population, demography (ie, population structure) and various health and cost indicators.

1.6 PRIVATISATION

(a) The privatisation of bodies such as the National Freight Corporation, Royal Ordnance, British Steel and British Gas has been a key part of the philosophy of the present Conservative government. This strategy has had many policy aims including the following.

The sale of public sector bodies and their associated assets produces cash receipts which are paid into the Exchequer. The government is then able to use the receipts either (i) to reduce taxes or reduce government borrowing and debt or (ii) to spend on some other public service: for example, the launch of the British Steel Corporation in November 1988 raised up to £2.5 billion.

A second policy aim is that privatisation is expected to make the services become more efficient as they have to operate in a market place. This increased competition should be reflected in a service more responsible to consumer wants at lower prices and offering greater choice. This is a difficult aspect to illustrate as there is frequently evidence of declining standards; for example, the office of Telecommunications (Telecom's regulatory body) still finds serious dissatisfaction with the telephone service in such areas as accounts, directory inquiries and consumer complaints. On the other hand, BT has raised the serviceability of public call boxes and has cut down the time taken to restore services.

A third aim is to provide the privatised services with a clearer definition of their role and objectives. Political influence is removed and their services are accountable to their shareholders and the capital markets. Thus the prices of an essential service like gas are no longer determined by the Secretary of State for Energy but reflect the competition in the market place. British Gas management could clearly plan for the next five or ten years of investment and need worry less about the political consequences of a change of government.

A final aim was to encourage managers and employees to become more committed to and involved in the privatised company's operations. It is perhaps easier to change working practices, to alter management structures and to introduce new technology to the privatised British rail subsidiary (Traveller Fare) than to the whole of British Rail. Certainly, if increased profits in any way reflect such changes, organisations such as Cable and Wireless have shown significant improvement.

(b)   If organisations can opt out of the public sector and/or become self-governing, the following advantages might accrue.

(i)   The organisation can organise and create its own management structures so as to deliver high quality services. For example, in hospitals, resources could be concentrated more on quality of service such as improved out-patient appointments. These revised structures should encourage faster decision-making to the benefit of patients.

(ii)   Local pay scales and conditions of service can be established by the organisation. They could give real power and responsibility to people working in a hospital. Skills can be more easily rewarded and higher quality staff can be more easily retained and become committed to the organisation. Thus Whiteley Council regulations on pay and conditions might not constrain the remuneration of employees in a hospital opting out of the NHS.

(iii)   Locally managed schools can foster local ownership and pride. Local business people can become involved with the government of the school as can parents. This local involvement allows the organisation to respond and react to local demands and needs.

(iv)   The capital assets of the organisation can be more effectively acquired and managed. Thus a hospital opting to become a trust can own its own assets, borrow to finance new buildings and deploy the assets to encourage their most effective use in improving patient care. The constraints of central capital controls can be relaxed and the need to compete with rival bids rests mainly on the ability to raise finance.

(c)   A problem of breaking down the coherence of the public sector arises when co-ordinating requests to central government. At present, there are national bodies such as the Association of County Councils who can lobby for extra funds. This co-ordinated planning and petitioning becomes more difficult as the number of independent bodies increases.

Secondly, national standards for health care or education become more difficult to define, maintain and monitor. Health care quality could be substantially above or below an acceptable standard set by the remainder of the National Health Service.

1.7   NATURE, ENVIRONMENT AND FUNCTIONS

The public sector is comprised of different organisations which not only contrast with those of the private sector but also have characteristics which distinguish one from another. Such organisations are clearly influenced by their distinctive nature, environment and functions. Thus civil servants at the Department of Social Security attempt to administer the social security benefits system by providing a helpful, accurate and prompt service to recipients and potential recipients. This meeting of a social need contrasts with the work of nationalised industries such as the Post Office and British Rail which operate in a more profit orientated manner, eg, in 1988–89 British Rail achieved a profit (before subsidy for services deemed socially necessary) of £304 million, mainly through property development transactions.

Central government influences the structure, environment and functions of the public sector. In particular the government provides major funding of public sector bodies directly via the grant system. Thus local government receives both the revenue support grant to finance services at a local level and also specific grants to be spent exclusively on services such as the Police Service. The National Health Service receives a majority of its funds via the Resource Allocation Working Party to provide hospital and community health services whilst separate monies are made available to support the Family Practitioner Services.

Political influence plays a major part in the operation and functioning of public sector bodies. For example when the Chancellor of the Exchequer makes the Autumn Statement he/she clearly identifies not only the total expected level of public expenditure analysed by department but also those programmes which have political priority such as expenditure on housing, the environment, education, law and order, etc. These priorities reflect the political idealogies of central government. Such political influence is also felt at a local level by the decisions and plans of locally elected and/or appointed members. The situation can be compounded if the political views of central government are the opposite of those held by local members. The paid officers frequently spend time attempting to reconcile the operational consequences of such differences.

At a very fundamental level the organisation and functions of the public sector are determined by statute. This means that the public sector can only undertake services for which it has statutory powers. Thus the Local Government and Housing Act 1989 specified how local authorities should conduct their business and administration. It attempts to ensure (i) that the voting membership of most committees is spread among the political groups on the council in proportion to the size of those groups and (ii) that local authorities should designate a head of paid service – usually the chief executive; such a post cannot be occupied by a designated chief finance officer who has specific financial responsibilities given by the Local Government Act 1988. The doctrine of 'ultra vires' prevents local government from acting beyond the powers specified in statutes.

Finally the control of many public sector bodies is difficult because it is difficult to measure the quality of a service as opposed to the quantity or cost of the service. One problem is that individual measures cannot assess quality of service; for example if a library has a system which identifies where a book is and can notify the reader it is available it may see itself as being effective, however the reader may interpret effectiveness in terms of the speed with which book requests are satisfied. To control and organise service provision it may be necessary to collect information from the local community on their satisfaction with services and their desired levels of service.

1.8 GOVERNMENTAL ROLES

(a) A minister or Secretary of State is involved in the making of policy for a particular department and for its subsequent implementation by civil servants, local government officers, etc. For example, the Secretary of State for Social Security heads the Department of Social Security. His primary function is the creation and implementation of welfare policies covering such matters as pensions, income support, and so on.

The minister creates policies in conjunction with other Cabinet colleagues based on the party manifesto. The policies are included in Parliamentary Bills which are enacted into legislation by Parliament and the Royal assent of the Monarch. The minister plays a vital role in co-ordinating government policies (eg, overall planning for services such as housing education, health).

In addition the minister will be responsible via the Department of Social Security for planning and monitoring social security requirements and standards at a local level; in this the minister is assisted by senior civil servants led by the Permanent Secretary who ensures policies are implemented and provides continuity in the department's administration as governments change.

The minister is responsible and accountable to Parliament for the actions of his/her department. Thus the Secretary of State for Social Security can be questioned by Members of Parliament on both their policies and the operational performance of their departments.

(b) Select committees consist of approximately fifteen members of the House of Commons; the composition of their membership reflects the party composition of the House. They include such committees as the Public Accounts Committee, the Treasury and Civil Service Select Committee which produce reports arising out of an examination of departmental accounts and the general financial management of departments.

Such committees might be assigned to specific departments such as defence, transport, health, etc. The committee monitors policy creation and its implementation. Other committees such as the Treasury and Civil Service Select Committee, are responsible for overseeing the government's economic and monetary policy in addition to managing and controlling the Civil Service.

The select committees can take written and oral evidence from interested parties; this will lead to the production of reports with published recommendations. The government can choose whether or not to implement the recommendations but the surrounding publicity and debate ensures some measure of accountability. Thus whilst the report might not produce any changes the select committees draws the attention of the House of Commons to matters of concern (eg, the financial policy of a nationalised industry).

(c) The National Audit Office is the department of the Comptroller and Auditor General. Officers of this department audit the government's appropriation and trading accounts (ie, the spending of monies voted by Parliament). Thus the officers auditing the accounts, certifying their correctness and reporting the results back to Parliament. The office has a key role to play in ensuring the stewardship and accountability of public money. Their reports are examined by Parliament and where necessary responded to by central government.

The Audit Commission, established in 1983, is a corporate body appointed by the Secretary of State. The key task of the commission is to appoint the external auditors of local authorities in England and Wales. Their second key task is to undertake studies for improving the economy, efficiency and effectiveness of local authorities. From 1990 the commission assumed similar responsibilities for the audit of regional and district health authorities.

The commission is independent of local government, its officers and members are not civil servants so that although the Secretary of State appoints the members he/she has no direct control over the commission's day-to-day activities.

The commission produces an annual report which is submitted to Parliament for scrutiny and debate. The equivalent body in Scotland is the Commission for Local Authority Accounts in Scotland.

1.9 PUBLIC SECTOR FINANCE

(a) The following diagram represents a typical finance department structure:

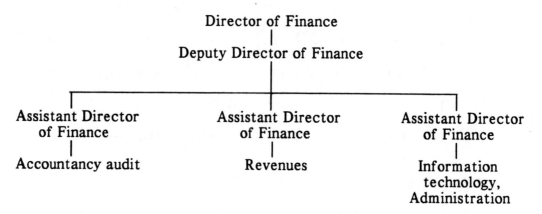

Accountancy – Payments, investments, budgets, accounting, costing investments.

Audit – Systems, probity, value for money.

Information technology – Control input, programming, systems analysis.

Administration – Secretarial support, personnel, reprographics central purchasing.

(b) The basic coding system usually comprises an objective code (ie, into services, divisions of service and sub-divisions of service). This is also accompanied by a subjective code which classifies expenditure into standard groupings and sub-grouping such as employee costs, supplies and services, premises, etc. The above structure can be illustrated in that expenditure on social services can be divided into that incurred on homes for children, elderly persons, handicapped persons, day nurseries, etc. It will also be possible to identify particular cost centres such as an adult training centre; the analysis will be able to split the supplies and services cost between provisions, clothing and equipment, laundry, etc.

Coding systems are required for reasons including the following:

(i) to assist computerisation of accounting systems;

(ii) to charge items of expenditure to agreed budget headings;

(iii) to identify costs which can subsequently be recovered (eg, via a grant claim);

(iv) to assist the production of management accounts (eg, job costs, cost centre analysis);

0144V

(v)   to process more readily the co–ordination of consistent and comparable financial accounts and statistics.

(c)   Records of fixed assets will include:

(i)   the location of the asset;

(ii)   the department and committee responsible;

(iii)   the authority for transfer and disposal of assets;

(iv)   classification of fixed assets (eg, land, buildings, equipment, apparatus, machinery);

(v)   value, method of valuation and date of last valuation;

(vi)   depreciation and write–off policies, where appropriate;

(vii)   responsibility for checking the inventory;

(viii)   internal audit's role in inventory control.

2   MANAGEMENT – POLICY AND STRUCTURE

2.1   FINANCE COMMITTEE

(a)   In most public sector organisations the committee responsible for finance is known as the 'committee of members' or indeed the Policy and Resources Committee. The purpose of this committee is that of discussing detailed financial matters which would normally not be considered appropriate for a board to discuss. These more detailed financial matters will include standing orders, financial rules and regulations and all the duties, responsibilities and delegation which go along with those areas.

The committee itself comprises a combination of groups, which might include the following:

(i)   chairs of other major committees within the organisation;

(ii)   business or financial experts;

(iii)   members from each geographical area in which the organisation is involved;

(iv)   members' representation proportionate to the political balance of the main body;

(v)   members who are randomly elected or selected.

The composition of the committee is important for it can be said that its effectiveness and power depends to a certain extent upon the person of the chairman and its members.

The functions of the committee are derived from its responsibility for the financial management of the organisation. The position and nature of the committee is such that it is able to consider **all** financial proposals and organise for the maximum utilisation of limited financial resources within the boundaries of the organisation's overall plan and objective.

The functions which derive from this include examination of various budgets, capital and revenue, long and short term, and the setting of fees and charges at appropriate rates. The committee is also responsible for examining control related aspects of financial management and also questions relating to borrowing, new financial legislation, use of funds, etc.

(b)   The chairman of the committee of members must perform the following duties:

(i)   submit items for inclusion in committee agendas;

(ii)   conduct and control the committee meetings;

(iii)   meet and consult with the principal officers within the organisation with the aim of collecting information and resolving problems;

(iv)   make decisions on issues delegated by the committee;

(v)   represent the committee as its spokesperson at other meetings;

(vi)   represent the finance view at other committees.

(c)   The roles of the members and officers are complementary and are perhaps best compared by means of two lists.

First, the role of the members is as follows:

(i)   taking major policy decisions;

(ii)   making specific decisions concerning the attainment of plans and objectives;

(iii)   general allocation of the limited resources of the organisation;

(iv)   general direction and control of affairs;

(v)   setting objectives;

(vi)   monitoring progress;

(vii)   carrying out a review;

(viii) fixing various local taxes and charges;

(ix)   representing and assisting electors.

The role of the officers is as follows:

(i)   providing the members with information and advice to assist in decision–making;

(ii)   producing reports, evaluating alternatives when in the process of planning;

(iii)   the acquisition and management of land, finance and staff;

(iv)   performing duties delegated by the committee;

(v)   designing and executing programmes and plans;

(vi)   day–to–day work.

2.2   CORPORATE MANAGEMENT

(a)   Corporate management involves planning and operating the activities of a public sector organisation for the benefit of the body as a whole. As far as the allocation of resources is concerned the various sections and interests within an organisation are brought together where there is corporate management to decide upon priorities. This corporate approach is very different from the traditional approach to management which made little effort to decide upon objectives and policy and which allowed the various sections in the organisation to compete for the limited resources. It must be noted that corporate management facilitates a more efficient use of resources, ie, land, manpower and finance.

The corporate approach to management is pursued through a number of units or committees including a policy and resources committee; a performance review sub–committee and a chief officers' management team. Each of these committees has a particular function. The policy and resources committee is responsible for formulating objectives and then creating, coordinating and controlling the implementation of a plan designed to meet those objectives. The performance review sub–committee must examine reports compiled by officers on the progress of the policies. The chief officers' management team is led by the chief executive officer, an important figure in the corporate approach because he/she has no responsibility to any one department. The task of their team is to discuss the policies and make recommendations to the committees.

The corporate approach does vary a little between authorities. For example, some authorities have created directorates where two or more departments have merged under one chief officer. Other authorities have argued that directorates are too large to manage effectively and have returned to more but similar departments under separate chief officers. In other organisations the chief executive officer has been dispensed with altogether.

(b)   Corporate management has a number of strengths when it is operated in a public sector organisation. First, it enables the optimum allocation of the limited resources which are available to the organisation. Second, because it allows for optimum allocation of resources, it facilitates greater efficiency and greater value for money. The corporate approach enables an earlier identification of the problems within the organisation as a whole. A final strength which can be noted is that corporate management creates a tendency for forward planning procedures to be improved rather than just looking one year ahead all the time.

The corporate management approach carries four major weaknesses. First, it is expensive to operate as it involves more meetings. Second, corporate management may exist in name only, for individual officers or members may still dominate decision–making, etc. It is evident that in some public sector organisations politics is so all–important that it rules over all other considerations and consequently corporate management just **does not** work. Finally, where services provided by one organisation overlap with those provided by another the corporate approach cannot work effectively.

2.3   ROLE OF OFFICERS

(a)   The management of many public sector organisations is usually shared between paid officers and elected or appointed members. Whilst it is very difficult to be prescriptive as to the respective roles of both parties it is possible to establish a framework for the member/officer relationship. Local circumstances are likely to alter the exact balance of such a relationship. The variations on the management and administrative themes are many. No two authorities are likely to work in precisely the same way, much will depend upon the degree of delegation to the paid officers. This answer will now proceed to examine the officer/member relationship in a local government setting.

Local authorities are traditionally based on a structure of committees comprising elected members supported by paid officers. This usually involves:

(i)   grouping related services under one committee eg, Library and Leisure, thus reducing the number of committees and making co-ordination easier;

(ii)   increased delegation to committees, chairpersons and officers to divorce policy decisions from execution and administration;

(iii) creating a Policy Committee of senior members to deal with major policy and co-ordinate the authority's work overall.

Within this structure members who are elected to the authority and officers who are employed by the authority operate generally within the following guidelines.

(i)   The control of the affairs of the authority rests with the members who should take key decisions on the objectives of the authority.

(ii)   The elected member will undertake periodic reviews of the progress and performance achieved by the authority.

(iii) The paid officers are responsible for the administration and case work.

(iv)   It is the duty of paid officers to identify particular problems and cases which, in their view, require a decision of members.

(v)   The guiding principle is usually that issues are dealt with at the lowest level consistent with the nature of the problem. Putting these guidelines into practice should mean that paid officers are given maximum responsibility whilst members are relieved of the day to day trivia eg, approving staff appointments below the level of deputy. On the financial side this can mean financial regulations which allow chief officers to spend up to the amount included in the annual estimates without recourse to the elected members.

The above description will have explained that elected members are responsible for formulating the strategy and plans of a local authority. This will involve the clear definition of the authority's objectives and a timescale for their implementation. The objectives will be communicated to the paid officers whose responsibility will be to implement such objectives. However the role of the elected member does not end at this point; it is important that the elected member monitors progress and ensures that the objectives are successfully implemented. The officers can be seen as being concerned with the operationalising of the policies made by the members. In other words officers must acquire and deploy the correct mix of resources to achieve the objectives. This will frequently require officers to advise members that there are insufficient resources – land, finance, manpower etc – to undertake a policy. Indeed it may be necessary for an officer to point out that there is no legal basis for undertaking such a policy.

In the above description there will obviously be areas of overlap. However there is one role of the elected member which is not the province of the paid officer and this is the constituency role. Here the elected member ascertains the views of his/her constituents and feeds such views into the policy making process.

To summarise, the elected member should be concerned with determining priorities and plans and allocating financial resources to achieve such objectives. The paid officer advises members and implements the authority's plans, the progress of which is monitored by both members and officers.

(b)   There are several administrative arrangements which can be mentioned in this context. The more important ones are given below:

(i)   The setting up of a finance committee or policy and resources committee to oversee the finances of the authority. This committee does not represent any one service but is rather a committee which weighs up the claims of the various departments for a share of the authority's limited resources. This evaluation will be undertaken in the light of the authority's overall plants.

(ii) The use of committees in general to establish the overall plans and priorities of the authority and its departments. In all these committees it is likely that officers will be called upon to advise members on the implications of their decisions.

(iii) As mentioned in answer to part (a), it is essential to have a scheme of delegation to chief officers which allows decisions to be made at the lowest possible level. These schemes of delegation lay down the relationship between officers and members in certain instances eg, supplementary estimates, virement etc.

2.4   POLICY MAKING

(a)   The processes involved in making the policies of public sector organisations varies not only between organisations but also within the same organisation. The process of deciding what the organisation ought to be doing in terms of the mix, level and scope of its services can be termed the policy making process. The question refers to the most common method of policy making namely the incremental approach which accepts the existing level of service and plans only for small changes from year to year. This answer will begin by outlining the key strengths of such an incremental approach.

(i)   The incrementalist approach recognises that predicting future events from very limited information is no easy task. Thus whilst an incrementalist might recognise the strengths of other more complex policy making models, the incrementalist would also appreciate that complex models require long term accurate data which is frequently not available or if it is, the data is incomplete. Short term changes with a relatively small impact are thus better to predict and control.

(ii) This first advantage is reinforced in the minds of many incrementalists by the fact that the policies that public sector organisations can pursue are severely restricted. Public sector organisations are limited in that they cannot act 'ultra vires' or 'beyond the powers'. This means that the policies of public sector organisations must be specifically allowed or sanctioned by an Act of Parliament. This constraint means that there is little scope for changes in policy other than an incremental approach.

(iii) The incrementalist approach is conservative in its approach to change and this should result in fewer serious errors of policy. Change is slow and its effects are predictable; such characteristics appear to suit elected members who are only too aware that mistakes may reflect on their showing at the ballot box.

(iv) A further strength is that the comparative simplicity of the method means that less time is required to produce a policy. This means that the process can be viewed as cost effective in terms of the results it produces as compared to the resources the approach expends.

(v) The small amount of time required is suitable in a public sector environment when information on which to base future policy is frequently not available until well into a financial year. This is particularly true of the level of financial support which Central Government is to provide.

On the other hand an incremental approach does have several weaknesses including:

(i) The approach fosters existing policy as this is frequently never questioned; this invariably means that 'poor' policy or errors are continued from year to year. The only part of policy to come under any serious scrutiny is the change at the margin and its effect on resources.

(ii) Because all the emphasis is on the marginal changes there is little time spent on defining the overall goals and objectives of the organisation. The emphasis is frequently on the inputs as opposed to the outputs the organisation would like to achieve.

(iii) Linked to point (ii) above is the fact that the incremental approach concentrates on short–term objectives as opposed to the longer term objectives. The incremental approach is ideal for 'fire–fighting' or problem solving as opposed to meeting longer term objectives. Thus an incrementalist might suggest employing security guards to combat vandalism on a housing estate whereas a more comprehensive solution might involve defining a policy for recreation and leisure facilities for children under fifteen.

(iv) The above three criticisms can be summarised in the fact that the incrementalist approach lacks the systematic approach to policy making. It does not encourage a value for money approach in terms of fostering economy, efficiency and effectiveness.

(b) There are a multiplicity of perspectives on what is rational or logical. For example an economist might say that to be rational is to select from a group of alternative strategies the strategy which maximises output for a given input, or minimises input for a given output. The aim of the rational approach is to avoid decisions being taken solely on personal grounds. Thus the policy makers will require information which will help to clarify policy problems, outline practical alternatives and their consequences and generally assist in decision making. This approach can be expressed as consisting of various activities which are outlined below.

(i)   A problem which requires action is identified, and objectives and values related to the problem are classified and organised.

(ii)   All important possible ways of solving the problem or achieving the objectives are listed; such alternatives are termed strategies, policies or courses of action.

(iii)   Predictions are made of the important consequences which would follow from each alternative course of action. It is important to assess the probability of such consequences occurring.

(iv)   The consequences of each strategy are compared with the goals and objectives identified in (i) above.

(v)   The preferred strategy is implemented.

(vi)   The implementation of the strategy is monitored to provide a constant feedback of information and so allow policies to be amended in the light of experience.

2.5   COMMUNICATION

(a)   The sending or exchanging of information, comments, etc, is what is understood by the term communication. It is the passing on of ideas to a recipient so that he understands the idea. Thus it is essential for the recipient and the sender to arrive at the same interpretation of the information as a result of the communication process. Effective communication will certainly involve the recipient understanding the language and/or jargon of the communication medium. Likewise the appropriate medium, eg, a telephone or a report must be used to convey the information. The language and terminology comprising the medium must be concisely and clearly expressed so that the information cannot be misinterpreted. The information must be comprehensive and not selected by the sender to mislead the recipient.

(b)   Quite simply the absence of the conditions identified in answer to (a) above will result in ineffective communication. These points can be illustrated by the following comments. There could be problems in the relationship of the recipient and the sender. The sender may not be trained or experienced in the art of communication. The recipient may just ignore and not act on the communication because he is not motivated to do so. There may be a personal grievance or dislike by the senders of the recipient or vice versa. The most common reason for failure, however, is that the recipient does not understand or misinterprets the communication of the sender.

The other basic reason is because the organisation structure does not facilitate effective communication. This is because there may be an absence of clear channels of communication, or because the working environment is oppressive or noisy. Again the distances between the recipient and the sender could lead to ineffective communication, eg, personal professional relationships can be more difficult to establish if the communication medium is continually impersonal, eg, reports or letters.

(c) The first medium to be considered is the telephone which can be used to contact members of the public or officers in other departments. There are variations on the telephone such as a telex system or the use of electronic mail. All involve a mechanical or electronic device which overcomes the physical distance between the recipient and the sender. They are quick methods of communication but they can be expensive to install and maintain. The telephone is a little more personal than the telex but does not provide a tangible record of the matters discussed. Furthermore, the physical distance does not allow the two parties to pick up the non-verbal communication signals such as gestures and facial expressions which can clarify the spoken word.

The above method can be contrasted with a second method of communication, namely, the written word in a report, a letter of a memorandum. These all provide a permanent record of the communication process, however, the written word lacks the personal contact which allows ideas to be expanded and discussed. Similarly comments and sentences written by the sender are liable to be misinterpreted by the recipient and can convey a different tone to that intended. Letters, etc, take time to produce, transmit and action and thus lack the speed of the mechanical medium. Finally, reports can be too detailed or arrive too late so that the recipient does not act on the content of the report.

A final method of communication employed by accounting technicians is face to face discussions. This might be at a committee meeting or in a visit to an officer in a service department. This method of communication allows written words to be supported by verbal explanations. This allows misinterpretations to be minimised and queries to be clarified more rapidly. The verbal skills of the sender and the recipient are critical to the success of this medium, thus accounting technicians may need training in how to present an argument at a committee. Thus it is possible for meetings to be ineffective because points are talked about but decisions are not made or information is not transmitted. Usually, however, verbal communications are planned in advance with agendas being prepared and the subject area being researched by both the recipient and the sender. This can make the face to face verbal discussion a more effective means of communication.

2.6 THE THREE Es

(a) Value for money in the public sector is frequently judged by determining the economy, efficiency and effectiveness of a product or service.

Economy is to do with avoiding waste, in acquiring acceptable and adequate resources in the lowest possible cost. Thus it is a little more than acquiring the cheapest resources but rather the appropriate quantity and quality of resources at an economic price. Thus schools could provide cheap school meals but they might not provide the appropriate nutritional level thus they could not be said to be economic.

Efficiency is concerned with the relationship of inputs to outputs. Put another way it is the capacity of a public sector organisation to produce measurable results in proportion to the resources used. Thus efficiency is concerned with maximising output for a given set of inputs or with producing a given level of outputs at the minimum cost. For example, in a hospital inputs can be measured in terms of numbers of doctors, nurses, bed spaces, drugs consumed, etc. However, outputs are more difficult, eg, patients cured or bed days can be measured but making clear the relationship between inputs and outputs is more complex. Thus changes in public attitudes to smoking may decrease lung cancer just as much as putting more resources into cancer research. It is often difficult to separate these effects and obtain a clear measure of efficiency.

Effectiveness is when service objectives are examined with a view to trying to gauge the degree to which they have been attained as a result of the service activity. In hospitals, for example, formal experiments can be set up to measure the effect of a particular drug or treatment service. Again in the education service effectiveness studies may be concerned with maximising consumer satisfaction as this is frequently the measure for gauging the worth of such a service. This requires objectives to be specified and generally capable f being quantified so as to allow objective evaluation. However, this is not always possible without some form of compromise, for example, the health service may set itself the objective of improving the health of the nation but how is this to be measured – what level of sickness or mortality is commensurate to a healthy society?

To sum up, the public sector can be economic and efficient without necessarily being effective. Thus the objective of reducing waiting lists in the health service need not necessarily be achieved just because the service is operating efficiently and economically. The three aspects of a service, namely, cost, quantity and quality are all interrelated and contributable to value for money.

(b)   Unit costs identify the cost of providing one unit of service or producing one unit of a product. Thus authorities are able to calculate the cost per citizen of providing a service, or the cost per meal served or cost per mile of street cleansed or weekly cost per place occupied amongst others. These are all indicators of efficiency and can be compared to pre-determined targets. The source of most comparative statistics in the public sector is the Chartered Institute of Public Finance and Accountancy which allow unit costs to be compared. However, statistical comparisons serve only as a pointer to possible differences in service efficiency which may or may not be borne out by further investigations. Differences exist between authorities in geography, population structure, quality and level of service provision and local demand – all of which affect costs.

Thus to give a more complete impression of an authority's performance and service delivery comparisons of unit costs are frequently accompanied by tables of service measures over a number of years. This allows the user to identify more general trends and to go 'behind the accounts'. Thus the education service might support unit cost figures with information on pupil/teacher ratios, number of schools, number of full-time equivalent pupils, employees per 1,000 population, etc. This approach gives a more comprehensive and balanced view of service provision. The unit costs by themselves tell the user little about the quality of the service provided, in fact unit costs concentrate on the economy and efficiency aspects of value for money at the expense of effectiveness. There is a danger that high unit costs may be viewed as being ineffective when because of the authority's needs the costs are more than acceptable. Conversely, high unit costs are often seen as being a reflection of an effective service in that the more one spends the better the service provided. Both these examples highlight the danger of using unit costs incorrectly.

Finally, unit costs are prepared by different authorities over periods of time. Thus it is not inconceivable that their accounting policies will change over time or differ between authorities. Such differences mean that unit cost comparison should be handled with care. They should be viewed as a means of highlighting areas for further investigations rather than providing definitive answers.

2.7 FIVE TERMS

(a) Span of control is the term given to the number of subordinates a manager can control effectively. This ability will obviously vary with, amongst other factors, the nature of the job being supervised and the managerial responsibilities and abilities of the supervisor. Similarly the actual time and the limitations of the human brain in dealing with several items will restrict the span of control a manager can effectively undertake.

In the public sector it is difficult to set precise numbers as to what is an acceptable level for the span of control. Thus in an internal audit department a team leader's span of control will depend greatly on the quality of the team leader and his/her subordinates. If the audit team is a cohesive group with several years' experience it is likely that they will perform a great deal of the management coordination which might otherwise fall on the team leader.

On the other hand the creditor payment section or payroll section of a public authority is frequently managed by one individual with a great number of staff in his/her span of control. This is often because the work of the subordinates is such that they perform identical tasks, eg, invoice checking and coding which are not interdependent. This independence of the tasks facilitates a larger span of control. The aim in the public sector should be to achieve a span of control which does not produce excessive levels in the organisation and does not unduly hinder the ability to coordinate activities.

(b) Corporate management attempts to manage the activities and functions of a public sector organisation as a whole, with a view to meeting a particular objective, eg, care of the elderly, elimination of an illness, etc. The aim is to recognise that activities are interrelated and to break down departmental barriers. For example British Rail may have corporate objectives which include the provision of safe, efficient and profitable operations for the conveyance of passengers and freight. This objective will require that all parts of British Rail such as the catering, rolling stock, track maintenance, research and development departments, know their part in achieving the overall objectives.

In practice the above approach is difficult to achieve as both officers and members in the public sector tend to be associated with functions and/or departments rather than with wider objectives. Thus many devices have been created such as central policy committees, management teams of chief officers and the appointment of chief executives or general managers all meant to generate and foster a corporate approach. These have all had limited success because altering structures is not the major pre-requisite of successful corporate management; rather it is necessary to alter individuals' aims and philosophies to those which recognise the organisation as an entity attempting to satisfy the disparate needs of the community.

(c) Delegation is one of the essential principles of organisation management; it is a process whereby an individual (or group) transfers to another individual (or group) the duty of taking particular actions or decisions. This delegation does not however allow the superior to relinquish the responsibility for the effective performance of the duty by the delegatee. Thus in the public sector the director of finance is responsible for detailed finance transactions of the authority. The director alone is not capable of carrying out all the finance functions, therefore delegation is essential. Thus accountants will attend committees and give financial advice in the name of the director of finance. Similarly decisions on investment patterns, audit programmes, income collection will be taken by staff of the finance department through the authority delegated to them by the director of finance.

At another level in the public sector it is usual for elected or appointed members to delegate to paid officers. This avoids the members becoming too involved in trivia and allows them time to concentrate on their key roles of policy-making, objective setting and allocating major resources; the paid officers need to receive delegated authority which allows them to implement such policies and objectives.

(d) Internal check is an essential part of management's internal control procedures. It involves the structuring of duties and responsibilities so that employees provide an automatic check on each other's work. This process will minimise the risk of fraud and error unless there is collusion between two or more employees. Thus in a district health authority the responsibility for authorising, handling and recording transactions for the purchase of drugs would be separated. The aim should be that no one employee should be able to authorise an action, have custody of assets acquired by the action and be able to record the accounting aspect of the action. Internal check procedures should be established by the director of finance and verified by internal audit. Thus the internal auditors need to satisfy themselves as to the adequacy of internal checks and that staff are complying with them to a satisfactory level.

One of the criticisms of internal check systems in the public sector is that they encourage employment of excessive numbers of staff; however, effective internal check should not encourage excesses because each employee is involved in a different aspect of a transaction and is not checking the work of other employees. The audit and examination of work is the function in the main of internal audit.

(e) Employee appraisal is a method of assessing the effectiveness of employees in the performance of their particular jobs. This is particularly important in the public sector which expends such a large proportion of its revenue budget on employee costs. The employee appraisal system needs to be both objective in its methodology and recognised by both management and employees. Frequently employee appraisals will form the basis for management decisions on promotions, training programmes, salary increases, bonus payments, etc.

The aim of employee appraisal is to measure employees' actual performance against expected performance for a particular job. This can assist managers in taking corrective action and also identify weaknesses and strengths of particular employees. This will usually involve managers in assessing the quantity and quality of work performed, the person's job knowledge, their communication skills, their leadership qualities, etc, as appropriate to a particular job. This obviously necessitates a job description setting out the main duties and the specific tasks and objectives, against which performance is assessed. Managers must also provide some form of forward job plan which sets out the peformance requirements during the next reporting period.

To summarise, employee appraisal is an essential part of the management process. Staff can only function effectively if they know what is expected of them, how success or failure is measured and what their managers think of their performance. Similarly, accountable managers must know who is doing what, where improvement is possible and in general how efficiently and effectively their subordinates are operating.

2.8   ZBB/CLF

Zero–based budgeting is a system which requires managers to justify their entire budget requests in detail. The reason why the expenditure is necessary needs to be clearly explained by the manager. In addition the benefits resulting from the expenditure need to be itemised. This can involve managers preparing budgets for different levels of activity; for example, a minimum level of service provision plus a series of separate decision packages identifying the costs and benefits of additional increases in activity. This approach allows the legislature to compare and determine priorities. The benefits of such a system include the following.

(a)   It provides detailed information on which decisions can be made to implement the organisation's objectives.

(b)   Managers will improve their efficiency as they must continuously evaluate their performance vis a vis the objectives of the organisation.

(c)   Previous levels and patterns of expenditure and service provision will be questioned and perhaps replaced by a more appropriate mixture.

(d)   ZBB requires the clear identification of objectives and aims from both politicians and senior managers in the public sector. Other systems of budgeting do not encourage objectives to be defined.

(e)   ZBB does not perpetuate existing inequities. It makes no prior assumptions, each increment of expenditure above zero is justified on its own merits.

The **Consolidated Loans Fund (CLF)** is an administrative device to avoid 'ear marking' of loans to individual capital projects. All loans raised for capital purposes are pooled in a CLF. Advances are made from the fund to finance capital spending on individual projects. Advances are repaid to the CLF usually by annual instalments over fixed periods. Interest and other expenses are also recovered annually. The CLF charges interest for borrowing services at the average interest rate over the fund as a whole.

Four benefits of such a fund include:

(a)   Loans can be raised on more favourable terms: the size and period of loans will be substantial as they reflect total borrowing needs of the authority.

(b)   The cost of borrowing is equalised over services. Previous borrowings at low interest rates can cushion current borrowing in times of high interest rates.

(c)   There is no need to identify individual capital projects with specific borrowings thus reducing the administrative costs of the fund.

(d)   The perpetual inflows and outflows of the fund mean that repayment of advances are available to finance new capital schemes.

2.9 PLANNING, DIRECTING, ORGANISING AND CONTROLLING

(a)   Planning of necessity precedes the other three activities of effective management. Plans identify goals to be reached and usually are quantified in monetary terms via a budget. Plans may be in the form of statements of intent by elected members on matters of fundamental and long-range significance to the local authority. They will be concerned with the services to be delivered and the resources – finance, manpower, land, buildings, etc – required to implement such plans. The timescale of implementing a coherent community care programme, for example, might be part of a health authority's plans. These plans specifying clear goals should influence significantly the direction and organisation of the authority in the future.

Plans need to be implemented and this involves ensuring that all the members of the organisation work together to achieve the defined goals. Communication will play a crucial part in directing subordinates as to their role in implementing the plans. The staff will have to have the appropriate skills, training and resources, and if the present balance is inappropriate senior management will have to direct procedures to redress the balance. This may involve recruiting staff with specialist skills such as information technology or alternatively retraining existing staff in new skills. Directing involves explaining or pointing out the way subordinates need to perform; it thus involves giving advice, guidance and supervision to all members of the organisation.

Organising is where management makes the best use of human resources both from the viewpoint of the individual and of the public sector body. Jobs to be done need to be identified and the right persons appointed to the jobs. It is also essential that management ensures that the individual jobs are co-ordinated to allow achievement of the organisation's goals. Decentralisation and delegation have a key role to play in effective organisations.

Control means more than measuring performance; it is necessary for an individual's performance to be related to the goals identified at the planning stage. This will involve management in setting detailed objectives for members of staff and communicating these objectives to staff. Control can only be facilitated if standards and targets are expressed in detail and not left in the form of long-term corporate goals. Actual performance can then be appraised in detail and the results communicated to the responsible manager. The variance of the actual from the standard needs to be explained in terms of its cause and corrective action taken by the appropriate manager. This action could involve reorganising the staff, changing working practices, training the staff or perhaps revising the plans and objectives in the light of experience.

(b)   An accounting technician will be appointed to a specific post in a public sector organisation, eg, a senior audit assistant in a local authority. This post might require the technician to report to the group auditor and act as a leader of a small team responsible for specific audit tasks such as fraud investigations, systems audit, etc. In order to carry out these tasks there will be a need for the technician to have authority to take action or make decisions; without this authority the technician would be unable to direct the team members. The responsibility for managing the team will be given to the technician but should the team members perform poorly it will be the technician who is responsible. However the ultimate responsibility for the audit will probably rest with the group auditor who is responsible for the actions of his/her subordinates, such responsibility cannot be delegated to subordinates.

2.10   INTERVIEWS

(a)   The following would be useful at the interview:

(i)   job title of the individual to whom the accountancy assistant is responsible and the number of staff that will be responsible to him;

(ii)   job grade, conditions of service and career prospects;

(iii)   brief description of overall purpose of job in relation to the authority, the finance department and the section;

(iv)   principal tasks to be carried out by the accountancy assistant in order of importance (eg, definition of tasks such as budget preparation, maintenance of accounts, etc, and their respective deadlines for completion);

(v)   details of any special aptitudes or skills needed (eg, use of information technology, communication skills).

(b)   Consideration of the timing, duration and location are important and must be agreed in advance. Reception arrangements and a tour of the office are also important. All interviewers should be clearly briefed as to their respective roles. Each should receive a copy of the applicant's application form, any references received and a pro forma checklist for scoring the candidate's performance across a range of skills, attributes and characteristics.

The aim of the interview is firstly to assess whether the candidate is suitable for the job and secondly to ensure the candidate understands clearly the terms and conditions of the job.

The interview would begin by introducing the panel and telling the candidate about the authority and the job. Using the application form, a biographical approach could be adopted, progressing naturally through their work experience discussing why they accepted each position, what they did and what skills and knowledge they had acquired. The recent experience of the candidate should be explored to find out why they feel the vacancy is an appropriate move for them. Brief references will be made to salaries and other conditions of service but detailed discussion will take place if a provisional offer is made. At the end of the interview, time will be allowed for candidates' questions and to draw the interview to a natural conclusion, probably after 35 to 40 minutes. The interviewing panel will then compare opinions and come to a decision to appoint, if there is a suitable candidate.

(c)   The following interview record form (see page 51) should be used to assess a candidate's performance. The six assessment criteria to be assessed are given below.

Education and training – The qualifications possessed by the candidate should at least include membership of the Association of Accounting Technicians; other relevant qualifications should be assessed (eg, diplomas in information technology). The dates and method of study should be noted.

Relevant experience – Gather details of previous jobs including their duties and responsibilities. The progress made in the job and particularly significant contributions to improving the job. Probably seeking a candidate with a minimum amount of post qualification experience.

Knowledge and skills – Detailed knowledge of the current legislation and working practices required by the post–holder. Clear and accurate responses of candidates to technical questions essential to the job. Has the knowledge been applied or is it the result of good interview preparation? Other skills required may involve reasoning ability, verbal ability, leadership, information technology skills, etc.

Personality/motivation – Assessment of the candidate's overall appearance, manner and speech. Particular personality characteristics will involve leadership, self–reliance, sociability and motivation. Why is the candidate attracted to the vacancy? What has he/she discovered about the organisation? Has the candidate a clear career pattern? Is this job a logical step? Does the candidate ask intelligent questions? Will they fit in?

Communication skills – Is the candidate able to comprehend a situation quickly? An ability to communicate orally with senior managers is essential. The quality of the application form should be assessed as written communication skills are also relevant to the job.

References – Two referees must be provided. Referees of character should be treated with caution and perhaps not considered until after the interview to confirm or contradict the interviewer's assessment. Use references mainly to confirm factual information of the previous job, period of time in employment and if relevant the reason for leaving.

For each of the assessment criteria interviewers should use the following rating scale: 5 = Outstanding, 4 = Good, 3 = Satisfactory, 2 = Fair, 1 = Unsatisfactory.

The ratings should be supported by relevant commentaries.

Interview record form	
Vacancy . . . . Candidate's name	
Assessment criteria	**Comments and rating**
Education and training	
Relevant experience	
Knowledge and skills	
Personality	
Communication skills	
References	
Overall recommendation . . . . Interviewer's signature . . . . Date	

3 FINANCIAL CONTROL AND MANAGEMENT

3.1 WORKING BALANCE

(a) The expected expenditure and income of an organisation is forecast in the one year revenue budget. However, expenditure and income patterns do not always match throughout a year; sometimes expenditure exceeds that forecast and provided for by the budget due to a number of unforeseen circumstances and in those situations income from elsewhere is needed. The working balance can be utilised to provide that extra income, which can often be needed in the early months of a financial year. The main purpose of the working balance is, in fact, to temporarily meet the gap between income and expenditure.

(b) The working balance may be affected by excessive expenditure, which can arise for a number of reasons. First, there may be unforeseen extra expenditure due to bad weather conditions remaining for a lengthy period. This will bring a need for expenditure in snow clearing, house repairs, etc. Inflation can also bring about an increase in expenditure above that forecasted if it rises above its forecasted level, as when inflation increases the prices of goods and services increase. The increase in prices, and therefore, in expenditure can be met by drawing upon the funds of the working balance.

An increase in the employer's National Insurance contributions or an increase in pension contributions due to legislative change will also often affect the working balance. Fourth, organisations may often have to take legal action to defend their interests, for example in trying to recover a debt or prosecuting for fraud; these actions can be costly if they are not covered by insurance and the working balance may be affected as it is called upon to cover the expenditure. Finally, increased capital allocations mid–year may result in higher capital expenditure which will affect the working balance of some organisations.

Even though budgets make provision for unexpected, increased expenditure, this provision may not be enough in extreme circumstances in which case the working balance is extremely valuable.

Just as expenditure may be greater than forecast, income may be less than expected for a number of reasons. First, services may not be used as much as expected and therefore the income expected from those services will be less than expected. For example, private beds in the hospital may not be used due to high charges, or the consumption of fuel may be reduced if the winter is a mild one.

Income from the community charge may fall short of expected returns for a number of reasons including non–registration, non–payment, delayed court action and an inability to pay.

3.2 CONTROL OF PAYMENT

(a) Financial control is a vital element in financial management. Without control there would be no effective, efficient use of the limited resources. The first step in exercising financial control is the production of a budget. A budget is, in effect, a financial expression of policy. A number of different officers within the organisation will then be given the authority to issue orders, although they must be careful to work within the limits set by the budget. To safeguard against error or fraud or irregularity the orders will have to be given by means of an official order form; only in an emergency can a verbal order relating to expenditure be given. Only regular or periodic payments such as rent, rates, etc, require no written orders; they can be made from an expenditure register. Those orders for other, 'extraordinary', items must be signed and completed with an expenditure code and estimated value, and a copy given to the organisation's financial department. Before any order is made the official responsible should take care to ensure that the expenditure is provided for in the budget and that the item being purchased is worth its cost.

After an order for goods has been made an invoice for payment is received. It is important that the official responsible for the order checks the invoice against the order for the following reasons. First, it is necessary to ensure that those goods which were ordered and invoiced have, in fact, been received. Second, the invoice itself needs to be checked for the accuracy of its calculations and also to certify that the VAT has been dealt with. Finally, it is important to check the invoice to ensure that the costs have been correctly allocated. This process of checking will often be performed by a number of officers to reduce the risk of error or fraud.

Authority for any order and payment must be obtained before a payment is made. This necessary authority may be given by a minute reference of chief officer's certification. Once the payment is made it is processed – most often by computer although checks will also be run by internal audit. The despatch of cheques should then be carried out by an officer who has not had any involvement in the payment procedure.

(b) (i) **Virement** – A virement is the authorised transfer of a budgeted sum from one budget heading which is underspending to another faced with an additional, unforeseen expenditure. The authority to approve such a move must be limited to a minimum number of people so as to ensure that the overall financial policy of the organisation is not eroded.

(ii) **Contingency** – It is important that a budget makes provision for possible unforeseen future liabilities. Such provisions are known as contingencies. It is difficult to forecast income and expenditure when inflation rates are volatile. In such a situation parts of the budget may be determined at the price level at a particular date and a global inflation contingency determined and held centrally. Positive control can then be exercised as this may be released when inflation becomes known.

(iii) **Financial commitment** – When an order for a particular good or item is made an organisation is financially committed. Financial commitment is therefore 'known liability'. It is important to record commitments to ensure that the expenditure is provided for within the budget.

3.3 INCREASING COSTS

(a) Rents, fees and charges have been generally increasing in certain public sector organisations to meet increasing expenditure due to inflation, VAT, etc, and to compensate for a fall in income from other services.

A reduction in government grants such as rent allowances, rent support grants, etc, has led to a reduction in income. The source of income has also been affected by the increasing difficulty for local government of increasing local taxation due to local electorate and political pressure.

(b) The provision of local authority housing since the Second World War has been regarded as of absolute priority until the election of the present government. Council housing is, therefore, a major local government service.

A number of factors need to be considered in calculating increases in rents, fees and charges within the housing department. The amount of rents used to be within the discretion of the authority but they must be reasonable and subject to periodical review. Reasonableness may be a question for the courts, which expect local authorities to act as trustees for the general body of local taxpayers and to balance this duty against that owed to a special class such as council tenants. A local authority has in theory to consider this balance as it assembles its budget prior to fixing the community charge.

Since 1 April 1990 and the reform of the housing revenue account and housing subsidy, the housing revenue account is 'ring-fenced'. This means that there cannot be any cross subsidy between housing rents and local taxes. This now means that housing rents cannot be subsidised by taxpayers and must therefore reflect the real costs of the housing provision.

Fees and charges should be renewed regularly taking into consideration expenditure and inflation. Any maintenance or repair work on housing that is rechargeable to the tenants should show the cost including administration being fully recovered.

The Housing Act 1980 determines the interest rate charged to mortgagors who purchased their council houses or flats and it tends to be the higher of the local average rate and the rate determined by the Secretary of State.

3.4   STOCK OF GOODS

(a)   Management needs to give consideration to a number of issues relating to stock. First, it is extremely important for a public authority to maintain stocks at a level which balances the costs of holding stock against the costs of being out of stock. Holding too little stock means that the demands of a department cannot immediately be met. Holding too much stock means that more funds are 'tied up' in goods than is necessary, which costs the authority additional interest charges. Overstocking will also lead to extra storage costs, obsolescence etc. If management is to control stock levels it is of vital importance that it is aware of the exact stock levels. Consequently it is most important to keep complete financial records of the stock situation and provision should be made for adequate insurance. The ordering and issue of stores should be the task of authorised signatories. Checks on the stock should made by the external and internal auditors as part of their audit.

Security is another major issue which needs to be considered in relation to stock. It is important that the security of the stock be facilitated: this can be provided for in a number of areas and in a number of ways. First, adequate security should be made against theft, eg, burgular alarms, security firms etc. A balance must be struck between the value of the stores being protected and the cost of the security system. Another security provision lies in the division of duties, eg, the ordering and issuing of goods should be separate functions; write-offs should be authorised by an independent authorised officer; also, the provision of internal checks is essential. Security is also facilitated by adequately trained stores personnel.

Security can also be provided for by financial rules and regulations which should designate responsibility for the stores with those responsible directly accountable to a chief officer. Finally, security will be facilitated if as few people as possible are allowed access to stock and the level and movement of stock must be monitored constantly and recorded.

(b)   The typical procedures for the ordering, receipt and issue of a stores item are as follows.

(i)   Check how much of this particular item is already held. This can be done by means of a physical count or a computer printout.

(ii)   Place an official order with the supplier.

(iii)   Receive the goods; here it is important to check the quantity and quality and sign the invoice.

(iv)   Store the goods in an appropriate place.

(v)   Receive a request for issue – this request should be certified.

(vi) Issue the goods by means of an issue note. The issue note needs to be processed through the stores accounting system.

(vii) Check the stock level with a view to preparing a new order.

3.5 VARIOUS ROLES

(a) The post of Chief Financial Officer to a public authority is a most important one. He holds primary responsibility for the financial affairs of a public sector organisation. He is responsible for managing the finance department which involves a number of duties as follows.

He is responsible for the preparation of budgets both for revenue and capital expenditure; he is also responsible for accounting systems providing all necessary management accounting information to members and officers; also for providing advice to various committees relating to financial appraisals. He is also responsible for providing a comprehensive computer service to all departments of the authority, both of a financial and non-financial nature. Due to the variety and sheer volume of this work the chief financial officer delegates to various subordinate staff. The qualified accountants to whom he delegates work are responsible for supplying him with information and advice and they also take responsibility as heads of various sections, services and functions.

(b) Qualified accountants are often responsible for a section or function within a public sector body. They provide financial advice, help coordinate budgets, work on project appraisals, supervise and train subordinate staff. Those qualified accountants who are section heads need to report regularly to the chief financial officer.

Just as the chief financial officer delegates to the qualified accountants so the qualified accountants delegate to the accounting technicians who carry out much of the work of a technical nature for the qualified accountants.

(c) The qualified accountant technician provides and prepares detailed accounts and other financial data for the qualified accountants and chief financial officer. This involves budgeting, costing and assisting in internal audits; providing financial and accounting information and credit control. Some accounting technicians may also have responsibility for controlling and supervising other staff.

3.6 LEISURE CENTRE

No service is free: it may be 'free' at the point of use but someone has to pay somewhere along the line. Thus when an authority is reviewing charges it is essential to strike a balance between the user and the taxpayer/ratepayer. In any review the starting point must be that of recovering the full cost including an apportionment of overheads and some acceptable return on capital.

There are two major reasons why charges should be subject to review and they are as follows.

(a) Inflation will create an increase in expenditure yet direct action is needed to adjust the income received from charges in order to meet the extra expenditure.

(b) Charges need to be reviewed regularly to tailor supply with demand and thereby maximise the income.

0144V

'Pricing policy' is the primary factor which needs to be considered when reviewing the charges for a leisure centre. A commercial organisation might review its charges on the basis of a need to make profit or more specifically to achieve a target profit. This is **not** the case for a local authority; the pricing policy of a local authority will **not** be based purely on the profit making motive. The pricing policy of a local authority is instead based on a number of factors or criteria. The first of these is the desire to maximise the use of the facilities and linked with this, to encourage use by designating specific categories of user. The pricing policy will also be based upon requirements for the charges to contribute a certain percentage towards employee and running costs; or to cover debt charges – or a combination of both. The desire to make a profit at a set rate will also influence pricing policy. Finally, politics is often a factor in establishing pricing policy: often the overriding issue in fixing charges is to reflect social policy which is a larger and more sensitive area. The reviewing exercise can therefore have quite different effects depending on when it is undertaken; few authorities, for example, are likely to increase charges on popular facilities close to an election.

It can be noted that whilst it is advisable to have aims on which prices are to be based, it may not be possible to achieve those aims immediately, but at least the establishment of criteria can act as a spur to innovation and efficiency.

Information about the level of inflation affecting the leisure centre should also be considered when renewing charges. Another factor which needs to be considered is charges for comparable facilities imposed by private organisations or other local authorities.

Consideration needs to be given to the possible reaction of users when reviewing charges. Statistics on users – past trends on which to base future predictions – should be available; as too, should be the chief officer's opinion as to user reaction to charge changes, especially where it is thought there is likely to be 'consumer resistance' which will affect usage.

A final factor which should be considered when reviewing charges is the timing of the review. This can be critical if, for example, notices need to be prepared to inform the public of imminent changes. Receipting devices may need to be adjusted; and some charges may have to be introduced on specific days in the year, for example, season ticket fees generally need to be fixed at the beginning of the appropriate season.

3.7   BUDGET PREPARATION

(a)   A fundamental difference between private and public sector organisations is that the public organisation is related to its sources of finance by a budget, while the finances of the private organisation are moderated by market forces. Therefore, a great deal of attention is paid to budgeting in the public sector, while performance in the market place provides the equivalent focus for the private sector organisation.

The aim behind the preparation of a budget is to establish the revenue expenditure and income plans of an organisation and perhaps also to include proposals for capital development. Although the budget may be used to assess activities in retrospect at a later stage it is essentially a forward looking document. It is most important as a means of examining the priorities of the organisation with a view to seeking possible savings.

The preparation of the budget for a financial year is a lengthy process beginning when the organisation presents its estimates for expenditure in the forthcoming year to a central agency. The central agency not only consolidates these estimates into a total budget, but also calculates the revenue implications. The total budget is then presented to representatives of Parliament who order the central agency to make cuts and/or increase revenue to achieve a better balance between income and outgoings. The negotiations that follow, between the organisation and central agencies, go on until the deadline is reached. At this point the formal decision, which has to be made if services are to go on uninterrupted, is taken. That formal decision is made by an assembly of elected representatives in a very visible way that is preceded by a politically significant debate. It can be said, therefore, that the first step in budgeting takes the form of an interaction between the organisation, the central agency and a political decision maker.

The next step should be taken some nine months before the start of the year for which the budget is intended. Now the available resources which have been identified should be compared with the forecast of requirements. There will inevitably be a mismatch between resources and requirements and from this opinions need to be formed and decisions made by all the chief officers.

The main part of the budget process begins in the autumn; it is at this time that central government announces in detail its revenue for individual authorities. At the same time, information is given, although not always in a final form, on capital expenditure allocations. Then, once detailed information concerning revenue support grant is received by the local authority it can make a more detailed assessment of how resources will match likely expenditure, especially if there is a possibility it will be 'capped' in local taxation terms.

The process of budget preparation in a public sector organisation is very much a corporate exercise. Each individual chief officer will be responsible for a particular part of the budget, estimating, initially, the likely resource requirements for providing those services for which the chief officer is responsible; then, however, the collective effort is brought together and studied by all the chief officers in the management team.

It is evident that a budget must be built up from the bottom if it is to be successful.

(b) The chief financial officer has a very important role to play in financial control. First, he is responsible for internal audits which although not always concerned with control are frequently of a control type. The role of the chief financial officer in control is also evident in the fact that he provides a system of budgetary control which aims to compare performance against predetermined standards. This activity is most important in ensuring effective financial control in the authority as a whole.

3.8   WORKING GROUP

(a) A multi-disciplinary working group of senior officers, in effect, expresses the corporate approach of an organisation. The idea of corporate management evolved during the 1960s but began to take shape after the Maud Management Committee Report in 1967 and became reality after the Bains Report in 1972. Their emphasis was on creating 'interdependence' between departments and committees and to do away with the existing functional/ departmental independence. This radical approach suggested the creation of a corporate management team, led by a chief executive and composed of chief officers/directors as team members. The ultimate purpose of such a group is to enable the organisation to provide an improved service for the benefit of the community.

A public sector organisation is often involved in a number of public projects which involve a number of objectives and solutions. The diversity of these means that an inter-service approach is advantageous. The multi-disciplinary group embodies a variety of skills and experience, eg, legal, financial, technical, management, etc, which cannot be found in a single department and which makes possible a corporate, coordinated approach to the issues, thus preventing narrow professionalism and overdepartmentalism.

The multi-disciplinary group may be extended to include officers from other public bodies.

(b) Public authorities expend a large proportion of the nation's resources and this responsibility is discharged in a political climate, with the absence of a profit motive and in the presence of strong competing pressures for public money. The arrangements for finance and financial administration must therefore not only be sound, but must be seen to be so. Consequently the chief financial officer must be a member of the multi-disciplinary management team, with responsibility for contributing financial advice and information.

The chief financial officer may often not attend the team meetings but he is represented within the group by a finance officer. This is an important role because of the importance of correct handling of finance and also because most projects or problems involve finance. He takes on a number of responsibilities. First, he is responsible for ensuring that the financial implications of the organisation's activities are taken into account throughout the organisation. He is, therefore, responsible for providing the group with financial information and advice; also with financial statistics, accounts and reports, for example, cost benefit analyses. The finance officer is also responsible for ensuring that the group adheres to the financial rules and budgets and any standing orders. It is also the job of the finance officer to approve any financial systems ensuring their adequacy and efficiency.

The multi-disciplinary working group has to work with the limited financial resources of the organisation – resource allocation is therefore important. Overall control of resource allocation and the smooth running of the process needs objectives and strategies that are agreed by all – it is not only the task of the finance department. In order to make decisions with regard to resource allocation, however, the finance officer must provide good financial information and analysis of the financial consequences of different, alternative courses of action. He needs, in effect, to make recommendations as to how the organisation's limited resources can best be used giving the maximum effect and yet not overstepping the overall financial plan of the organisation.

3.9 CONTRACT TENDER

(a) In seeking a tender it is important that the organisation complies with its standing orders and financial regulations. The tenders should be sought by means of local and national advertising taking care not to overstep the regulations laid down by the European Economic Community.

In receiving and assessing a tender the organisation must follow a laid-down procedure. The tenders themselves must be in writing, enclosed in a plain, sealed envelope and returned to a designated officer. In seeking tenders an organisation will set a certain time and day by which tenders must be proposed. Until that set time any tenders which are received must be kept in safety by the receiving organisation.

The actual receiving or, more particularly, the opening of a tender must follow a set procedure. Each tender must be opened in the presence of members or officers prescribed in the rules and as each tender is opened it must be endorsed and a record kept of the tenderer and the amount.

It is important that all the tenders should contain full details about the work, the duration of the contract, the price, the provision relating to liquidated damages and that they should offer sufficient security for due performance.

A thorough assessment of the tender must be made before acceptance. An arithmetical and technical examination needs to be carried out and the financial standing and experience of the tenderer should also be checked. The financial provisions of the tender are most important and it is the job of the chief financial officer to ensure that they are clear and fair. The price fluctuation clauses and use of the price index formula need to satisfy the CFO and the tender must specify retention sums, payment of interim monies and the final account. The damages and penalties clauses must be acceptable as must the security, any insurance cover and the variation provisions.

The rules of an organisation specify which people in the organisation can accept a tender – the determining factor in this being the value of the tender. No tender, other than the lowest, can be accepted without a written report from the appropriate officer.

(b)   The chief financial officer is responsible for recording certain information relating to the tender in a contracts register. The authorisation of expenditure should be recorded by the CFO in the contracts register and also the variation orders. The interim accounts should be paid on a certificate from the technical officer responsible and the due dates for the payment must be specifically observed. An audit of the final account should be made before payment.

3.10   COST–BENEFIT ANALYSIS

(a)   Cost–benefit analysis is the measurement of the total cost of a scheme against the total benefit gained from that scheme. The benefits, it must be noted, include not only the financial but also the wider social and economic benefits.

A cost–benefit analysis can be made by first examining the costs and then the benefits, finally bringing all the factors into common terms.

The costs of a scheme to be examined can be grouped under the following three main headings.

(i)   **Direct costs** – in the form of capital costs or loan charges.

(ii)   **Indirect costs** – for example, travel expenses.

(iii) **Intangible costs** – for example, the inconvenience caused to road users by a lengthy closure of a main road. Such costs are very difficult to assess but are important if the cost–benefit analysis is going to be accurate.

The benefits can also be examined in terms of direct benefits, indirect benefits and intangible benefits.

A number of difficulties must yet be dealt with even after an examination of both costs and benefits have been made. It is important that a distinction is made between genuine costs and benefits and 'transfers'. Second, it is important to make sure that all the relevant factors have been examined. Third, it is important to set a 'cut-off' point as the possible effects which might be considered are often limitless. Finally, if a cost-benefit analysis is going to be effective the list of costs and benefits must be reduced to a form in which it can be totalled and assessed. This can be quite a problem in that the interest rate chosen is crucial if the cost-benefit analysis is interested in producing an absolute value.

(b) When finances are not readily available to a public sector organisation it often cannot carry out a full programme of capital works. In order for a choice to be made concerning which projects will be undertaken priorities need to be determined. Each project needs to be considered and by means of the cost-benefit analysis technique the net benefits and credits can be examined.

Cost-benefit analysis is also useful for public sector organisations if a choice needs to be made between two projects which have the same or similar objectives. It can be said that cost-benefit analysis is useful because it aids better decision-making, although it must be noted that the legal and political constraints which act upon public sector organisations restrict the beneficial effect of cost-benefit analysis with regard to decision-making. Finally, it can be said that the usefulness of cost-benefit analysis for public sector organisations is very dependent upon the skill with which it is carried out especially in terms of evaluating the intangible.

3.11 EXPENDITURE

(a) Capital expenditure is financial outlay for goods and services which are of long-term use or benefit, ie, more than one year. Expenditure coming under the definition of capital expenditure would be expenditure on the acquisition of land, vehicles, immovable plant and machinery, the construction, repair, improvement of buildings and the making of grants of a capital nature.

(b) Anything which is not capital expenditure is revenue expenditure. Revenue expenditure includes those costs which relate to the year of account and so, therefore, whilst the purchase of a car would be capital expenditure, the cost of road tax, petrol, etc, would be revenue expenditure.

(c) The three major sources of finance for public authorities' revenue expenditure are:

(i)   fees and charges;
(ii) local taxation eg, community charge; and
(iii) central government grants.

Revenue expenditure can be financed by fees and charges. These are of two types: 'point of sale' fees, for example, car park charges, swimming pool charges, dental charges etc, and those which are nationally determined, eg, planning applications. In order to meet inflation, many fees and charges have recently been increased, as have rents where they were previously unusually low. In the case of charges for key social services, the charge is calculated by means of an assessment scale. Assessment scales are sliding scales of charges for a service for individuals who, because of low income, would otherwise be discouraged by cost from accepting an essential social service. It normally involves the authority ascertaining the amount of income the applicant has available to meet the charge after taking into account their various commitments.

A second source of finance for revenue expenditure is local taxation in the form of the **community charge**. The community charge is a flat-rate charge on all residents within the local authority area aged 18 years and over. Each year, local authorities produce estimates of likely expenditure for the coming year.

From this figure they deduct their estimated income from charges and central government grants together with any cash balances available for the purpose. This leaves a balance which then has to be financed through locally levied taxation.

The third source of finance for revenue expenditure, central government grants, has since 1 April 1990 taken the form of **revenue support grants** (RSGs).

Revenue support grants (RSGs)

The RSG is a straightforward system with two major differences from its predecessor, the rate support grant.

(i) RSG is distributed on the basis of the government's view of what each local authority should spend (ie, for spending at the level of assessed need). There is no attempt to vary grant entitlements upwards or downwards in relation to changes in spending.

(ii) The tax base is different: instead of aiming to produce a common rate poundage across the country, the new system is designed to produce a common tax per adult across the country.

Specific and supplementary grants

Finance may also be forthcoming from the Secretary of State in the form of specific or supplementary grants. These may be percentage, unit or block grants.

The largest specific grant is the Police Grant which meets 51% of approved spending. Other examples are Urban Redevelopment, Slum Clearance, Public Transport, National Parks, Housing Benefit and Improvement Grants.

Internal funds may be used to meet revenue expenditure, such as the capital fund. When all sources of income have been taken into account, remaining net expenditure must be paid for from local taxation (community charge).

3.12 DIRECT CHARGING

(a) In parts of the public sector such as the electricity, gas and water industry, direct charging for services has always been the major source of finance. Central government grants have, however, been a key source of finance for other public sector bodies such as the National Health Service and local government. In recent years these grants have been reduced or have risen little in real terms and consequently those organisations dependent on them have been forced to increase their proportion of revenue raised by means of direct charging. As far as local government is concerned it has been facing a two–fold problem in that not only have grants from central government been effectively reduced but it has been unable to compensate for those cuts by increasing local taxation due to recent government legislation restricting the level of local tax increases. Consequently direct charging has become an increasingly important source of finance.

(b)   Several factors need to be taken into account when fixing charges for services.

First, consideration needs to be given to the type of service which is being provided, ie, is the service being provided for socially desirable purposes, eg, meals on wheels, or is it commercial and therefore requiring a return on the capital?

A second factor which must be taken into account is the effect of price increases on the demand for a service. For example, if train fares are too high will fewer people use the facility, thereby creating diminishing returns?

Another consideration lies in the fact that statutory provisions may prohibit an increase in the charge. For example, prescription charges are centrally determined.

Political considerations form a fourth factor which is taken into account. For example, if a local election is approaching the elected members will not want to lose votes because of price increases.

The pricing policy of the private sector is an important factor especially when the public sector organisations are competing with the private sector for work.

It is important to ensure that the cost of collecting the income generated by direct charges is not too great a proportion of total revenue.

Two final factors which need to be considered are as follows. It is important to examine whether a reduction in price would create a demand for a service which the public authority was unable to meet. Consideration should be given as to whether it is physically possible to limit access to the service so that only those who pay for the service will be able to enjoy its use.

It is important to note that profit is not the sole motivation for the setting of service charges but that wider social or economic objectives often play an important role in fixing the level of charge.

3.13   PROJECT FACTORS

Several factors should be included in a report to a committee which is to deliberate upon whether a project should be included in a capital expenditure programme. They are as follows:

(a)   The project should be described **fully** in the report to the committee.

(b)   The aims and objectives of the project must be stated and the case **for** the project, ie, its necessity, communicated to the committee members.

(c)   The priority level of the project should be established for the committee and the consequences if the committee does not give its approval to the project.

(d)   A detailed schedule of the capital cost should be presented to the committee, so that they can appreciate the full extent of the commitment if they choose to approve the project. This capital cost will include such things as professional fees, equipment, building works, furniture, etc.

(e)   A plan of how and when the capital will be spent over the time period of the project must be presented to the committee. This is important to enable the chief financial officer to plan his financial strategy and to ensure that there is a full utilisation of capital expenditure allocations.

(f)   In order to allow the chief financial officer to plan his borrowing strategy and cash flows the sources of finance for the project need to be specified.

(g)   Key dates in a contract should be identified in order to monitor progress. Such key dates will include tenders, land acquisition, contract duration, etc.

(h)   The committee should also be presented with information relating to manpower requirements in order that there can be some kind of manpower planning.

(i)   The total revenue costs must be detailed and also information regarding the phasing of those costs. Included in revenue costs are wages, debt charges, establishment expenses. If any income or cost savings are going to be generated by the project, this should be pointed out. The overall effect on net expenditure should be shown along with the effect on the revenue budget and the local taxpayer where applicable.

3.14   RISK AND REPERCUSSIONS

(a)   Financial vetting of contractors prior to awarding a contract entails an examination of the financial viability or standing of the prospective contractor. There are no set procedures for financial vetting but it will entail a financial assessment of the contractor either by employees of the public authority or by a private firm experienced in such matters. In many authorities it is a requirement of being allowed to tender or accept a contract that the relevant financial information to allow the vetting to take place is made available by the contractor. The basic documents required are usually the contractor's accounts over a period of years and banker's references.

The aim of financial vetting is to try to highlight the possibility of the contractor going into liquidation; in other words to establish that the contractor has the financial resources and expertise to complete the contract. This necessitates using historical accounts to predict the contractor's financial performance in the future. This is usually achieved by calculating appropriate accounting ratios in order to obtain a basis for evaluation. This evaluation will compare the contractor's performance over a period of time and occasionally with similar firms in a particular industry. The ratios usually cover various areas but in particular examine profitability, liquidity, capital gearing and the efficiency of the firm in utilising their assets. The aim of this process is to try to detect a pattern or trend in the financial performance of the contractor in these key areas.

Financial vetting based on accounting ratios must be used cautiously. The ratios are merely indicators and are not of themselves a basis for decisions. For example, they are based on historical data taken on one particular day of the year and should be treated cautiously. It will frequently be necessary to discuss one's findings with the contractor's accountants to probe any areas revealed by the ratios. There are after all perfectly good reasons for many poor accounting ratios, eg, cyclical trade, etc. Overall, financial vetting attempts to reduce the risk of selecting a financially unsound contractor.

(b)   Performance bonding is a type of insurance which the authority requires the contractor to take out prior to issuing the contract. It is an attempt to reduce the financial consequences of a contractor going into liquidation. The contractor enters into a contract with a bank or specialist firm that in return for a fee the firm will guarantee to reimburse the public authority for loss (or a proportion thereof) arising out of a liquidation. Frequently the bond covers a percentage of the value of the contract, say 10%. The contractor usually includes the premium in the contract price.

Performance bonds will not be required with every contract. The chief financial officer must consider the following points:

(i)   the extent of the potential loss that the authority could incur if a bond were not required;

(ii)   the opportunity cost of the performance bond;

(iii) the extent to which financial vetting has been carried out on the contractor;

(iv)   the previous experience of the contractor.

Overall the authority should attempt to assess the financial repercussions of a liquidation as compared to the risk of a liquidation. Bonds will not usually be taken out for what the authority classes as low value contracts or for contracts which have a relatively low risk based on the results of financial vetting.

3.15   OFFICIAL ORDER FORMS

(a)   Examples of ways in which official order forms can assist financial control include the following.

(i)   Official order forms can minimise the possibility of a duplicate payment of an invoice and can be used to monitor part receipt of an order. This is because the order form should be marked off by the authorised officer as and when the invoice is passed for payment.

(ii)   The official order form can facilitate internal check. The person who raises the order should, wherever possible, be someone other than the person who receives the goods into stock. This means that more than one person is responsible for controlling the ordering and receipt of goods.

(iii) At the year end or even throughout the financial year outstanding orders can be ascertained to calculate a creditors figure or to establish the expenditure committed against a particular budget heading. This is particularly useful if commitment accounting is adopted as a basis for budgetary control.

(iv)   The official order form is a basic document for the internal auditor. It records the issue of order books and is a prime document in supporting expenditure, eg, is the order signed by an authorised officer?

(b)   The checks to be carried out on an invoice prior to despatching the cheque can easily be split between those of the spending department and those of the finance department. This division will of course vary depending on the size of the authority.

The spending department should verify the following.

(i)   The appropriate officer should verify that the goods or services invoiced have been received in the correct quantity and quality. This will be the officer authorised to verify invoices, and verification will be made from either the official order form or the goods received note.

(ii)   The receipt of the invoice should be marked on the official order form. This is particularly important when only part orders are received.

(iii)   The authorising officer should verify that the invoice has not been previously paid.

(iv)   The prices quoted on the invoice should be verified against the quotation, contract price or market price as appropriate.

(v)   Discounts should be taken where appropriate and invoices passed promptly to ensure that discounts are received.

(vi)   The invoice should be checked for arithmetic accuracy.

(vii)   The invoice should be verified as being legal expenditure for which there is adequate budget provision; an appropriate expenditure code should be inserted onto the invoice certification slip.

(viii)   Photocopies of invoices or statements should **not** be certified for payment; original invoices are to be the only source of payment.

(ix)   The authorised officer, having verified the above, should sign the certification slip and forward the invoice to the finance department for payment.

(x)   In all the above instructions the authorised officer is defined as the person responsible for the budget vote against which the invoice is to be charged.

The finance department should verify the following.

(i)   Verify that there is an authorised signature on the certification slip certifying that the above checks have been carried out. The signature should be verified from an appropriate list of authorised signatures.

(ii)   Briefly check that the invoice is arithmetically correct, that discounts and VAT have been correctly identified and that an expenditure code has been inserted.

(iii)   Briefly examine the invoice to see if the goods or services identified on the invoice are of a type that is commensurate with the work of the spending department.

(iv)   If any of the previous checks have not been carried out by the authorised officer return the invoice to the spending department. In appropriate cases, eg, to obtain a discount, information may be obtained over the telephone.

3.16   MANPOWER BUDGET

(a)   Manpower planning is the implementation of a strategy which attempts to achieve effective acquisition, utilisation, improvement and retention of an organisation's human resources. The manpower budget is a statement which brings together the expected implications for manpower of an authority pursuing a set of defined objectives. The budget can cover a period of time usually one to three years. A manpower budget is much more than a financial quantification of the costs of employing labour.

The steps involved in the preparation of a manpower budget are as follows.

(i)   The clear definition of the organisation's objectives and the ways in which such objectives are to be achieved. This should be done at an organisational and departmental level.

(ii)   The preparation of a forecast of the manpower in terms of number, type and hierarchy, required to operationalise the objectives. This can be looked upon as an assessment of the demand for manpower.

(iii)   An inventory of the current level and type of manpower available to the organisation. This process will necessitate an examination of the suitability of manpower in terms of such characteristics as education, training, skills, location and number of posts. This in effect is looking at the supply side of the manpower equation.

(iv)   A comparison of the demand for manpower in the light of the organisation's objectives, with the supply of manpower as identified in the inventory of manpower. This reconciliation should identify the action the organisation needs to take to ensure that the correct types of manpower occupy the appropriate posts at the time they are required. The type of action required will involve policies being established for recruitment, training and retraining, resignations, retirements and redundancies of staff. These policies should allow the manpower levels identified in the budget to be achieved at the correct time.

(b)   The advantages of preparing a manpower budget include the following.

(i)   The budget provides an inventory of the current supply of manpower in terms of numbers, grades, experience, capabilities, accommodation, etc. This is important as managers are better able to control the use of an important resource.

(ii)   The manpower budget can provide a basis for an accurate forecast of the organisation's manpower costs. This will be useful when preparing the annual revenue budget.

(iii)   The preparation of any budget requires that officers and members plan the organisation's activities in a coherent and systematic manner.

(iv)   The manpower budget will identify areas of expansion and reduction of manpower. This will allow managers to set up training and recruitment programmes.

(v)   The budget is subsequently an instrument for controlling and reviewing manpower throughout the subsequent periods.

(vi)   Overall the budget should lead to better value for money in that manpower should be utilised in an economic, efficient and effective manner.

(c)   The problems of preparing a manpower budget include the following.

(i)   The costs and difficulty of recruiting suitably qualified staff to prepare, implement and monitor a manpower budget.

(ii)   Many public sector organisations do not explicitly define the objectives of the organisation. This is partly to avoid being pinned down to particular policies and also because objectives in the public sector are difficult to define in concrete and measurable terms.

(iii) The basic records required to measure the supply of labour are frequently inadequately maintained. Organisations usually have information on numbers of staff but data on qualifications, career progress, skills and aptitudes is frequently less comprehensive or up to date.

(iv)   As with any budget there is a problem in forecasting the demand for a particular resource. Requirements for particular types of labour are continually affected by such factors as new technology, legislation, central government policy, finance, etc.

(v)   Whilst manpower budgets can be used to identify career paths and motivate staff, there will be a problem of introducing a new idea into the organisation. Departmental managers, employees and trade unions may not cooperate in the implementation of a manpower budget.

3.17   SOURCE OF FUNDING

(a)   This document is intended to explain the financial arrangements of 'XYZ' District Health Authority.

Introduction

The National Health Service spends in the region of £17,000 million in the United Kingdom and employs around 1.2 million full and part–time staff making it the nation's largest institution.

The Health Service is financed on a National basis from three main sources:

	%
Taxation	89
National Health Insurance Contributions	10
Patients' charges	1
	100

The National resources are allocated to Regional Health Authorities using a population–related formula which attempts to establish the need for health care. The long term aim of this process is to attempt to remove geographical inequalities in the provision of health care. The allocation of resources to District Health Authorities from the Regions is also by reference to a similar formula as described above but modified to take account of local circumstances.

Cash limits

In the NHS as with other public sector organisations, the method the government uses to exercise financial control is operated through the Cash Limit system. What a cash limit does is to restrict the amount of cash spent within an Authority over a given period with financial penalities should that limit be exceeded.

The cash limit allocated at the start of the financial year includes an additional estimate for pay awards and price increases that are likely within that period although should these increases be greater than the estimate, the Authority would still have to manage within that cash limit.

Cash limits can be divided into three different types of allocation:

(i)   Revenue – for day to day running of the Authority's services eg, nurses' salaries, catering, fuel, drugs etc;

(ii)   Capital – purchase of land and buildings, building works over £15,000, purchase of vehicles;

(iii)   Joint finance – for projects managed in conjunction with local authorities which may be revenue or capital.

Revenue expenditure

In a typical year the greater proportion of expenditure of 'XYZ' District Health Authority will be on salaries and wages – approximately 70% – with the majority of it being incurred on nursing salaries. The remaining expenditure will be spent on items such as drugs and medical and surgical equipment, provisions, fuel, light and power, and estate management. It is also possible to classify revenue expenditure in terms of that spent on hospital services and that spent on community health services.

Capital expenditure

'XYZ' Health Authority occupies about 100 acres of land and a wide range of buildings including hospitals, health centres, clinics, offices etc. The Authority receives a capital allocation to provide for a programme of minor capital spending. In addition larger capital schemes are submitted annually to the Regional Health Authority for consideration for inclusion within the major capital programme. In the NHS capital expenditure is defined as the acquisition of land and property; building and engineering schemes costing £15,000 or more; individual items of medical, dental and computer equipment costing £7,500 or more; all purchases of vehicles and the pay and expenses of staff who are fully or mainly engaged on capital work.

(b)   Two interested groups who might be interested in the document outlined in (a) above would be:

(i)   the members of the health authority; and
(ii)   the clients served by the health authority.

The benefits to be gained from using such a document will be common to both groups in many instances. The benefits could include the following.

(i) An improved understanding of financial jargon and terminology such as capital and revenue.

(ii) More educated users and managers in the NHS which could reduce misunderstandings etc.

(iii) The document could provide for promoting greater accountability in the use of public resources. This document could supplement the more comprehensive and detailed annual accounts.

(iv) The document could assist newly appointed members by quickly allowing them to comprehend the financial workings of the health authority. This will be of particular use when faced with financial reports.

(v) The document can be used by members to explain the financial background of the health authority to interested parties eg, the media, patients etc.

3.18 TENDERING

(a) Public sector organisations are frequently involved in a tendering process whereby they invite bids or prices at which goods or services will be supplied. This answer attempts to explain the differences between certain types of tender.

(i) Open tendering and selective tendering are two ways of inviting persons or organisations to tender. The key difference between the two methods revolves around the degree of restriction placed upon persons or organisations able to tender. Thus in selective tendering tenders are invited only from selected firms or contractors. The selected tenderers are chosen from a list maintained and compiled by the public sector organisation; it is not uncommon for names to be included on the select list after a financial and technical appraisal of the firm's capabilities has been undertaken. Again the select list frequently includes the names of contractors who have successfully completed work for the authority on a previous occasion. It is usual for the organisation's financial rules to stipulate a minimum number of tenders to be invited when adopting a selective approach.

An alternative approach is to have no restriction on the persons who are invited to tender, in other words to adopt an open tendering approach where any firm can respond to an advertisement to tender. The problem with this method is that it is necessary to fully appraise the background and abilities of the tenderers before reaching a final decision; this avoids authorities accepting the lowest tender which could be submitted by an inefficient organisation. This open approach however does facilitate accountability and can stimulate competitiveness.

(ii) Contracts can be either fluctuating price or fixed price based. With the former the contractor is allowed to adjust his/her prices in accordance with officially agreed increases in the tender rates. For example labour costs could be increased in accordance with national **union** wage agreements. This type of fluctuation is usually allowed via a 'rise and fall' clause included in the contract and is most frequent in contracts covering relatively long periods.

Fixed price contracts are where the price agreed at the beginning of the contract is likely to be the price paid. The word 'likely' is used because as with all contracts tender amounts can be varied up or down if there are agreed alterations to the Bills of Quantities or Specifications.

(b) The following are five examples of checks to be made by the Chief Financial Officer prior to paying an interim certificate on a long-term capital contract.

(i) The interim certificate should be an original document duly certified to ensure that the work to which the certificate relates conforms with the official contract and has been examined or approved as appropriate.

(ii) The interim certificate should be checked to ensure that prices, extensions, calculations, discounts, other allowances, credits and tax are correct.

(iii) The appropriate entries should have been made in the central Contracts Register; in particular that the interim certificate has not previously been passed for payment.

(iv) Ensure that the expenditure has been properly incurred, is within the relevant budget provisions and is in accordance with the Standing Orders, Financial Regulations etc of the Authority. This will entail checking the approval of the original contract amount together with any variation orders and/or price fluctuations.

(v) Ensure that the correct relation percentage is shown on the certificate and has been retained from the payment; retention monies are not normally released until an agreed period of time (say six months) after the contract is completed. Retention money is a provision should any of the work subsequently prove to be unsatisfactory.

(c) The key points to be included in the financial rules governing the procedures for the letting of contracts for goods and services would be on such matters as:

(i) the need to comply with the authority's financial rules;

(ii) the situations when competitive tenders are required prior to letting a contract; any exceptions to this should be clearly identified;

(iii) the methods of inviting tenders eg, open lists, selective tenders etc which are to be used and the circumstances in which they might be employed;

(iv) the procedures for the receipt and safe custody of tenders and records eg, plain envelopes, closing dates, nominated opening officers;

(v) the detailed procedures for opening tenders, particularly the need for two or more people to witness openings;

(vi) the rules governing the admissibility and acceptance of tenders eg, proper documentation, proven record of contractor, lowest tender etc;

(vii) the need to issue a formal legal contract with appropriate financial clauses covering such matters as liquidated damages;

(viii) the need to report all tender acceptances to the appropriate committee.

3.19 INTERNAL FUNDS

(a) The two types of funds which will be described are a Trust Fund in a district health authority and a Capital Fund in a local authority.

Health Authorities are empowered by Act of Parliament to accept, hold and administer gifts and legacies as trustees. These are known as Trust Funds, Endowment Funds or Non-Exchequer Funds. They may be used for any health service purpose or research project subject to any condition specified with the gift or legacy. They are frequently used for purposes for which the funds received from the Government to run the Authority are considered inappropriate, such as television sets for the wards and Christmas festivities for patients.

In general the types of expenditure incurred by a Health Authority on Trust Funds can be classified into the following three categories.

(i) **Patients' amenities.** Such expenditure might be to supplement that available from the Authority's Revenue Funds, but in most cases would be on expenditure not permitted from these sources, eg, television sets for short-stay patients, patients' trips, patients' holidays etc.

(ii) **Staff amenities.** Under this heading might be included all kinds of additional recreation facilities and entertainments for staff.

(iii) **Other hospital purposes.** Such expenditure might include that on both Capital works and Revenue Account which could, were funds available, be met from the Authority's allocation.

Hospitals and departments frequently receive donations from other organisations and the general public and this income has to be administered separately from the monies received from the DHSS. Charitable trust funds are, therefore, created to deal with these donations. The control of trust funds is governed by statutes and donations may only be spent for the purpose for which they are given.

It is sometimes the case that a donation is not spent immediately where, for example, an appeal to purchase a particular item of equipment is in progress. It is also the case that the terms of certain donations require the authority to invest the money and spend only the investment income. The statutes therefore allow for trust funds to be invested prior to being spent.

The types of investment vary from bank deposit accounts through to stocks and shares. Each of the donations, whilst remaining separately identifiable, forms part of an investment pool. Investment income in the form of interest, dividends and profits from the sale of stocks and shares is redistributed to each individual trust fund thereby increasing the amount of money available for spending.

Local authorities frequently establish capital funds; these internal funds may be used towards meeting capital expenditure or to provide for premature loan repayment. The fund is built up by making contributions to the fund annually out of revenue. In addition the fund is increased by repayments to the fund (both principal and interest) and income accrues from the temporary investment of the fund balance.

There are various ways of charging capital expenditure to the fund. Firstly, the fund may meet all the capital expenditure in one financial year with no requirement to repay or secondly 'advances' can be made to services and repaid over a specified period, with or without interest as the organisation determines.

It is an advantage to use the fund rather than borrow externally if interest rates are more favourable, also administration costs will be less. The fund may be used to effect emergency or opportune purchases without increasing the revenue budget if repayment is not required.

The fund is established under the Local Government (Miscellaneous Provisions) Act 1976 which allows such contributions into these funds as the authority sees fit.

(b)   Financial management of internal funds will be influenced by the following:

(i)   the statutory limitations placed upon the fund's investments; such limitations will be found in the Trustee Investment Act 1961;

(ii)   the need to maintain or increase the real value of the investment;

(iii)   the requirement to generate investment income;

(iv)   the necessity to maintain the capital or nominal value of the fund;

(v)   the need to invest the fund balances in a way that will minimise loss to the fund; generally losses are less likely if the balances are invested internally within the authority;

(vi)   the necessity to ensure adequate contributions are made to the fund to meet any known demands;

(vii)   accessibility to investments should be available as and when they arrive;

(viii) to utilise fund balances only for approved purposes, defined when the fund was established;

(ix)   to determine whether investment should be made internally or externally of the authority;

(x)   to decide what type of investment advice is required to manage the fund – this may require the services of an investment broker.

Overall the aim of fund management is to maximise investment income whilst maintaining the capital value and necessary accessibility at appropriate times.

3.20   MONITORING

(a)   A budget expresses the objectives or goals of an organisation in physical terms whether it is monetary, manpower, units of service, etc. Thus comparison of the budget and actual results forms the basis for evaluating performance and helps to control future operations. The control process allows corrective action to be taken to eliminate problems that are revealed in the comparisons. Actual performance is best measured by comparison with budgeted figures rather than past figures. Thus if budgets are reasonably formulated and based on all available information the budgetary control process facilitates effective implementation of the plans of the organisation. The key ingredient of budgetary control is not just identifying differences or variances between planned and actual performance, but rather identifying reasons for the variance together with the corrective action to remedy the variances.

(b)   The budget statement should be clearly identified with the cost centre or unit to which it relates. This should be backed up with information about the responsible budget holder and the period covered by the budget statement. These facts facilitate identification of the report and the officer responsible for controlling a particular budget head.

The type of expenditure and/or income should be identified (eg, cleaning materials) and this might be followed by the annual budget figure. This is necessary to confirm that this type of expenditure has been approved and included in the organisation's master budget.

The next column might identify the proportion of the annual budget available for this particular period; for example, one twelfth of the annual budget might cover a month. On the other hand it might be more useful to produce a profile of the expenditure/income particularly when it is subject to seasonal variations, eg, income at a swimming baths.

Finally it would be necessary to highlight the cumulative expenditure/income together with the cumulative proportion of the budget to date. This gives a more comprehensive view as variations in one period may be corrected in subsequent periods. The cumulative figures will identify this fact. This cumulative position would be shown in a final column identifying the cumulative variance and whether it was favourable or adverse. This can be more sophisticated and predict the annual variance should the present level or trend of activity be maintained.

(c)   The critical difference between commitment accounting and income and expenditure accounting revolves around the point in time the use or receipt of financial resources are recorded in the accounts of the organisation. Income and expenditure accounting records transactions at the point expenditure is incurred or income becomes due; this does not always correspond to the payment or receipt of cash. It thus involves adjusting accounts for expenses owing or prepaid or alternatively for income due or paid in advance.

Commitment accounting records transactions at a much earlier point, that is at the time financial claims and liabilities arise; this is frequently taken to be the point at which goods are ordered and services requested. This is achieved by estimating the value of orders and debiting them in the appropriate account and subsequently replacing this debit with the actual value of the invoice.

The income and expenditure method is useful for producing the accounts of the organisation in line with general accounting practice. On the other hand the commitment accounting method helps budget holders keep a more current check on their budget heads. This can reduce the possibility of overspendings because of outstanding orders not being accounted for in the income and expenditure method. The two methods cannot be ranked in terms of being better or worse than the alternative; rather the methods should be viewed as being appropriate for different purposes.

3.21   EXPLAIN TERMS

(a)   **Contingency provision**

A contingency can be defined as something likely but not certain to happen; something dependent on a probable but not certain event; in budgeting terms a contingency provision refers to an allowance for an event or circumstance which is either totally unforeseeable or else is forseeable but the extent of its occurrence cannot be accurately forecast.

This could cover such things as a the cost of clearing up a local disaster caused by the weather eg, a storm or more frequently a provision to cover pay and price increases during the budget period.

Contingency provisions are either controlled centrally by the Finance Committee or included in the specific budget headings. Whatever the method of control it is usual for approval to the use of contingency funds to be obtained prior to the expenditure being incurred. Thus departments/budget holders are required to justify the use of such provisions.

(b)   **Working balance**

The sum of the accumulated surpluses of income over expenditure is termed the working balance (eg, the total of the general fund, county fund or other funds of a local authority).

Such balances are necessary to finance ongoing expenditure prior to the receipt of income such as the community charge or central government grants. The balances can also be utilised by a local authority to lessen the impact of a proposed increase in the annual rate of local taxation.

The level of working balances is very much subject to technical information eg, debt collection period or creditor payment cycle, together with the political decisions of elected members; for example, the Council may feel it appropriate to run down the working balance in one year, whilst the balance might be increased in another year. This obviously has a major impact on the financing of a proposed budget.

(c)   **Financing capital expenditure from revenue**

The majority of capital expenditure in the public sector is financed by borrowing ie, a loan is raised to finance the asset and the debt together with interest is paid back over a period of time. The annual repayments, called debt charges or financing costs, are charged against the current revenues of the organisation.

On certain occasions capital expenditure is not financed by borrowings but rather by charging the capital cost entirely to current revenues. This policy will eliminate interest charges and debt management expenses. Such a decision is the exception rather than the rule as the decision means that large amounts of capital expenditure falls on current taxpayers. This is seen by many as inequitable because the expenditure will generate benefits to taxpayers over several years.

From a budgeting viewpoint charging capital expenditure to revenue results in wide variations from year to year and can result in considerable fluctuations in local tax rates. On the other hand debt charges tend to be at a constant level year on year and so assist the budgeting process.

(d) **Supplementary estimates**

When a budget holder wishes to incur expenditure not included in the original budget, approval has to be gained from the finance committee. This will require the submission of a report outlining the need and level of such expenditure. These requests are called supplementary estimates and can arise for several reasons eg, the introduction of new legislation; increased demand for a service, a change of policy by the elected members etc. In addition to such deviations from the budget supplementary estimates will be necessary to correct any miscalculations/errors in the original budget preparation.

Supplementary estimates while frequently necessary do disturb the balance of the original budget finances and for this reason should be kept to a minimum. Additional expenditure has to be financed either by the transfer of monies from another budget heading by increasing income or alternatively by using the contingency provision.

3.22   CODING

(a) A code is a series of numerical and/or alphabetical symbols which allow items to be classified or grouped together. The essential characteristics of a coding system include the following.

(i) Ease of understanding and use by the operator of codes, ie, brief but comprehensive.

(ii) Codes should be unique in that they classify one item throughout the organisation.

(iii) Codes should allow new items at a later time, ie, the code should be flexible.

(iv) The length and structure of codes should be uniform throughout the organisation.

(b) Codes in the public sector can usually be divided into an objective classification and a subjective classification. Thus the first section of a code would identify the cost unit or cost centre to be charged with the expenditure or credited with the income. This section is the objective classification. On the other hand the subjective classification of the code is that part which identifies the nature of the expenditure eg, salaries, heating etc. So for example if we take the coding system of a local district council we can illustrate the above. If we choose the environmental Health and Control Committee as an illustration.

Service Head: Environmental Health and Control

Division of Service: Environmental Control eg, food control, health and safety at work, pollution control, infectious disease control, general and community health.

Sub–Division of Service: 'X' market, 'Z' Depot etc

The above are the objective classification of the expenditure/income. This could be followed by a subjective analysis as illustrated below.

Standard Classifications: eg, employees, premises, debt charges etc.

Thus code 0120 1640 could represent the expenditure on food control at 'X' market being the national insurance cost of an employee.

Further sophistications are available such as characters denoting the financial year to which the expenditure/income refers or symbols which allow particular jobs to be costed within a sub–division of a service (eg, roof repairs to the civic market).

(c)   The benefits of controlling stock of materials in a public sector transport depot by the use of a coding structure include the following.

    (i)   The system will facilitate the production of cost accounts and financial statements both during the year and at the end of the financial period.

    (ii)   Coding systems, because they are relatively short, save time when dealing with items which have long technical names. This is particularly useful when receiving or issuing materials etc.

    (iii)   Coding systems lend themselves to computerisation with all the benefits; these would include the identification of slow–moving items, the monitoring of reorder levels, reorder quantities and other essentials of sound stock control.

    (iv)   The provision of a code provides a unique identity for particular items. This lessens the chance of errors when issuing items of a similar nature eg, types of screwdriver. The clear definition aids communication and recording of stock requirements.

3.23   NEW SOURCES OF INCOME

(a)   It is the head of the department, eg, a headmaster or a unit administrator who is usually responsible for the control of such funds; but he/she may delegate the day–to–day control to an appropriate member of staff.

The rules should be in writing and compiled with the help of the director of finance. The rules should include the following.

    (i)   The purpose of the fund should be clearly defined, ie, what type of expenditure can be incurred.

    (ii)   A member of staff should be appointed treasurer of the fund – responsible for all accounting records.

    (iii)   Auditors should also be appointed; generally two auditors (neither being the treasurer) would be adequate.

    (iv)   Audits should be frequent; chief officers should inspect the auditor's certificates.

    (v)   At the end of each period, say each month, the auditors should verify that the cash in hand and at the bank agrees with the cash book balance.

(vi) An annual audit should be carried out and cash book balance again verified, and receipts and payments checked as far as possible.

(vii) Where amounts are held on behalf of patients, pupils, etc (eg, trips and savings), it is strongly recommended that individual collection cards should be used. These cards should be collected from patients, pupils, etc, annually and produced for auditors to ensure that the total cash shown as being owed to patients, pupils, etc, is in fact in hand.

(viii) The auditors should verify the books, etc, as being correct as far as they can establish.

(ix) Possibility should be considered of investing funds, eg, in local building society or bank deposit.

(x) If an investment account is opened only designated officers, eg, the treasurer should be able to withdraw cash.

(xi) Receipts for all types of approved expenditure should be obtained and inspected.

(xii) An annual set of audited accounts should be presented to the staff or committee responsible for managing the fund.

(xiii) Overall the sound system of internal check should be applied so that no one person has total control of the funds.

(b) The key factors would include the following.

(i) Service departments must notify the treasurer's department of all debts to be raised as soon as possible after the goods or services are provided. Frequently this task is decentralised and service departments initiate the invoices.

(ii) Full details of the charges must be provided, eg, date, address, rate of charge, service provided, etc.

(iii) Invoices should be raised promptly; clear instructions should be given on the invoice of methods of payment.

(iv) Wherever possible pre–payment for goods and services should be encouraged. This is not always practical, eg, where the charge is based on time taken to perform a service.

(v) Proper systems of recovery should be installed, usually involving reminders being sent after an appropriate period, eg, four weeks.

(vi) Final reminders threatening legal action should be issued.

(vii) Legal action should be instituted if cost effective to pursue.

3.24 FINANCIAL CONTROL

(a) Financial control could be described as the entire management systems which an organisation employs to control its finances and ensure that resources are both acquired and employed with a view to ensuring economy, efficiency and effectiveness. Such control systems may be those employed internally such as internal audit or those applied by external influences such as cash limits.

Thus the overall aim of management is to keep expenditure under its control and to monitor the inflow of revenue so that the organisation will know whether its plans have been implemented.

(b) Five features essential to effective financial control systems include the following.

    (i)   A clear definition of the objectives of the organisation and of how each part of the organisation can help to achieve such objectives.

    (ii)   The defining of individual responsibilities for keeping within budgets, authorising expenditure and controlling income, in particular responsible officers in service departments, should be clearly identified.

    (iii)   The prime responsibility of the resources committee assisted by the director of finance for supervising and controlling the overall management of the organisation's resources, eg, by establishing budgetary procedures, organising the finance departments, etc.

    (iv)   The need to ensure that the financial consequences of all policies and plans are considered at the correct management levels; this will usually involve the director of finance being a member of the management team and being able to provide financial advice directly to the highest decision–making group or committee.

    (v)   The establishment of routine control systems to regulate such things as the custody of assets and stores, the submission of financial reports, the design and use of financial records, the provision of a centralised accounting system and the organisation of both internal audit and internal checks.

(c)   (i)   The National Health Service is subjected to cash limit controls and cash planning. A cash limit is the total amount of cash which can be withdrawn from the Exchequer in any financial year. It is basically a finite or absolute amount of money available to finance NHS revenue expenditure. This cash limit system was introduced in 1976 and initially attempted to maintain the 'volume' spent, ie, maintain service levels at their existing levels as any underestimate of pay and price increases was adjusted in the following year's cash limit. In 1981 a system of cash planning was introduced which basically said that the cash resources voted would remain fixed irrespective of the actual level of pay settlements and price increases. Thus volume of service was no longer protected as any shortfall of funding would have a recurring long–term effect.

    (ii)   In local government the powers and duties of the Audit Commission are an example of an external financial control. The Commission as we know it was established in 1983 as a result of the Local Government Finance Act 1982; this provided a statutory duty on the local government auditor to produce a code of practice with which the local government external auditor should comply, and a responsibility to ensure local authorities take proper steps to secure value for money, ie, economy, efficiency and effectiveness in the use of resources. The auditors of the Audit Commission have responsibilities for the financial and regularity audit as well as value for money studies. The auditors are required to report to the local authority and to publish their report and send a copy to the Comptroller and Auditor General who may lay the report before the House of Commons. This emphasises that local authorities are subject to the controls exercised by central government and its departments.

3.25 REVENUE BUDGETS

(a) The following points identify five reasons why public authorities prepare revenue budgets.

(i) The annual revenue budget is a statement which assists short-term planning. This provides a link between the planning and execution of the longer-term plans of the authority, and relates the short-term plans to the authority's declared objectives.

(ii) The budget is a means by which an accountable manager at every tier of management has a clear definition of his/her responsibilities analysed in terms of costs and revenues.

(iii) The budget provides a base for the control of income and expenditure. The overall spending of the authority can be monitored throughout the year so that corrective action can be considered in cases of variance between budgeted figures and actual results.

(iv) The actual revenue budget process can facilitate the most effective deployment of limited resources between competing programmes and/or services. For example a zero-based budgeting approach requires that every item included in a proposed budget must be justified and approved.

(v) The budget enables the cashflows of the organisation to be planned so that alternative sources of finance may be both assessed and actioned. This can be useful in fixing charges, levying local taxes, determining borrowing policy, etc.

(b) The example given is taken from a local authority; it should be emphasised that the exact methods and timing of procedures will vary between authorities. A most common procedure is based on the base budget approach which identifies the costs and revenues of continuing the current level of service. Any changes to this base are identified in terms of an improvement bid which represents the financial consequences of growth in the level of service provision or alternatively financial savings arising from a reduced level of service.

The base budget is usually made up of traditional elements of expenditure, eg, employee costs, running costs and financing charges. When preparing this base budget it is necessary to take account of salary increments, the revenue consequences of capital schemes, non-recurring items; for example, items specific to one financial year need to be deleted from the next year and finally full-year effects of service changes started part-way through the current year or pay awards granted part-way into the financial year. The above considerations are mainly controlled by the authority itself but there will also be external factors which are outside the direct control of the authority, eg, the impact of new legislation, which need to be taken into account in establishing the base budget. These figures are usually prepared by members of staff in the operational departments with the advice of the finance department. This process usually takes place between October and mid-November.

During November the service committees consider the various improvement bids and the financial savings put forward by the appropriate departments. These will be considered in the light of advice prepared by the director of finance and the resources committee on the possible levels of expenditure and income for the authority as a whole. This advice will be based on central government's expenditure plans, likely levels of working balances, projections of pay and price increases, forecasts of likely grant and income levels and the overall policies and plans of the authority.

During November and December the director of finance will coordinate and collate the base budget, the improvement bids and the financial savings. This process will usually involve discussions between the finance department staff and senior officers in the service departments. The aim of this process is to submit a detailed budget to the resources committee before or after Christmas when clearer information about levels of grant are available. The resources committee will discuss the budget and may ask the service committee to review their budgets again prior to agreeing a budget for recommendation to the authority. Thus in February/March the authority will set the precept or local tax level and approve the budget.

3.26 FUNDED v UNFUNDED

(a) A funded superannuation scheme is one in which contributions are made to the fund by both employer and employee to provide for future pension liabilities. The fund is invested in order to ensure that the fund grows at a rate sufficient to finance both current and future pensions, etc. Examples of such funds include local authority superannuation funds with the exception of those for teachers, police and fire service staff.

An unfunded scheme is one where pension liabilities are met from contributions during the year with deficits being covered by current contributions. These types of scheme are employed by central government for its employees, eg, those in the National Health Service. This type of fund relies on a topping up by government as and when required.

(b) Three types of income to a funded scheme are:

(i) Employees' and employers' contributions; employees' contributions are deducted from salaries/wages at an appropriate percentage rate. In addition the employer will contribute an amount to the fund to meet the employee's pension.

(ii) Income from investments both dividends and capital profits accumulate to the fund as a result of investing surpluses in equities and gilt–edged securities.

(iii) Transfer payments from employees transferring from another public body. This occurs when an employee takes up other pensionable employment and the fund pays a sum of money called a transfer value, based on the current actuarial value of the employee's pension benefits, to the new occupational pension scheme.

Three types of expenditure

(i) Pensions to employees; this is the benefit paid to employees when they retire from employment (eg, on reaching the age of 60) and have completed the minimum reckonable service. The pension is normally calculated at a rate of the average salary for each year of reckonable service; the pension is paid to the employee for the rest of his/her life.

(ii) Retirement lump sums; again on reaching retirement age and having the appropriate reckonable service employees will also receive a lump sum payment from the fund. This is calculated at a percentage rate of the average salary for each year of reckonable service. Average salary usually means the highest amount on the employee's salary for a successive 365 days of reckonable service (ie, service which counts towards the reckoning of benefits).

(iii) Death grants or gratuities; this is a gratuity payable to a deceased employee's personal representative (eg, the executor of the deceased's estate). Depending on whether the employee dies whilst in service or after having left the service, the size and terms of the gratuity will vary.

(c) Three main categories of investment are distinguished as:

(i) wider-range investments, eg, company shares, property investment, unit trusts;

(ii) narrower-range investments requiring advice, eg, government and local authority stock, debenture loans;

(iii) narrower-range investments not requiring advice, eg, National Savings Bank deposits, local authority bonds, National Savings Certificates.

The distinction is made to impose a limit on the mix of the fund investments so as to protect the contributors to the fund. The wider-range investment is very risky with the chance of wide fluctuations in both capital values and income; in fact neither increases in capital values nor regular income are guaranteed from this type of investment. The maximum amount of a fund which can be invested in this type of fund is 75%. Because of the risk involved advice must be obtained prior to investing in this category.

Similarly the second category – narrower-range investments requiring advice – carries some risk. This is because although the interest is guaranteed there is a real possibility that capital values will fluctuate. Thus the security is not 100% guaranteed.

In both the above categories advice should be given to the trustees by a person or group who has experience in the selection, buying and selling of investments. This could be through an investment panel, the director of finance, management consultants, stockbrokers, etc.

The final category of investment – narrow-range investments not requiring advice – comprises those where the investment is not at risk and the income is fixed and guaranteed. Because of the minimum risk involved no formal advice need be obtained by the trustees.

(d) An actuary is an individual or company who estimates the risks and probabilities in relation to the value of a superannuation fund. In other words the actuary assesses the ability of the fund to meet its future and current liabilities. If the fund is inadequate the actuary advises the employer to increase contributions to ensure the fund is topped up to an adequate level; the converse will apply should the level of the fund be seen as excessive by the actuary. This type of professional advice is obtained approximately every five years.

3.27   PUBLIC SECTOR CHARGES

(a)   (i)   Charges which are nominal are those which are small in size when compared with the cost of the product or service being provided; they are usually levied for political reasons such as subsidising the use of leisure facilities or services to the elderly.

(ii)   Charges which are determined by an Act of Parliament are termed statutory charges. Examples would be prescription charges, motor tax, etc. The charge must be levied by the public sector organisation in accordance with the law.

(iii)   A means-tested charge is one related to a person's ability to pay (eg, meals on wheels or sheltered accommodation).

(b)   A means test is a way of levying charges which takes account of a person's ability to pay. It is frequently employed to ensure that essential services are not out of the reach of individuals because they do not have the resources to pay the full cost. The user of a service is asked to supply details of his/her income after deductions are made for essential living expenses such as food and heating. The remaining income left after this process is used to determine what, if any, charge of a person should pay. Many of the income support benefits are assessed using this method.

(c)   Five essential features of a successful assessment scale:

(i)   The scheme should be quick and easy to implement in terms of producing prompt results for clients.

(ii)   The test should not be so complicated and full of red tape as to discourage potential applicants.

(iii)   The scheme itself should not generate such administrative costs as to make it better to provide a free service; the costs of collecting debts should not be too expensive.

(iv)   The scale should ensure that only clients with obvious need obtain a subsidised service; it should be remembered that the subsidies have to be financed from somewhere, usually other taxpayers or users of the service.

(v)   The scheme should be flexible so as to allow for special cases; red tape and standardisation are useful but should not dominate the means test.

3.28   PUBLIC SECTOR ACCOUNTANTS

(a)   Wherever accountants are located their primary function is to provide financial advice to managers; thus in a polytechnic the accountant will provide financial advice to the governing body, the Directorate and the many budget holders throughout the college. This will of necessity involve the accountant in the functions of financial planning, budget preparation, budgetary control, income generation, project appraisal, etc.

The above will involve the accountant in setting up financial information systems to meet the needs of managers; this will frequently involve identifying budget holders and cost centres. The collation and presentation of financial data which can be used to monitor actual financial performance against budgeted performance is another key task. The accountant will promote a cost conscious attitude to the use of resources by value for money and systems appraisals with a view to encouraging economy, efficiency and effectiveness. From the above it will be seen that the service department accountant is not usually concerned with the more routine financial procedures such as payroll preparation but rather with the strategic/policy–making procedures. Of course there will be exceptions where such routine procedures are part of the service accountant's responsibilities.

(b)   The key management issue raised by this question is the definition of who the accountant is responsible to. Being located in the service department is likely to mean that the accountant owes a loyalty to the departmental manager, yet the accountant's professional qualification may mean that strong pressures are exerted by the Director of Finance on professional matters.

This problem discourages many accountants from seeking out such a position. This uncertainty is fostered by the possible poor career structure in the service department where accounting support may be minimal and could result in the service department accountant feeling isolated. There is also the fact that if there is still a central finance department there could be problems of communication, eg, delays in the transmission of financial data from the centre to the service department. It can also mean tasks are duplicated in that the service department accountant re–works data produced by the central department and vice versa.

The management problems above suggest that clear job descriptions outlining responsibilities, reporting mechanisms and common interests are a prerequisite of any successful decentralisation of the accounting and finance function.

3.29   BUDGETARY FLEXIBILITY

(a)   Freedom to spend within a given fixed budget allocation is attractive to budget holders but can bring problems including the following.

(i)   Much of the public sector is controlled by detailed cash limits and figures imposed by central government. Thus it is necessary to know in advance the break–down of budgets as well as the total amounts in order that budgetary control may be operated effectively.

(ii)   Freedom within a single allocation can mean that managers take decisions without considering the consequences of such decisions. This can be the case when a decision this year commits the organisation to high expenditure in future years. Such commitments may not be in line with the future plans of the organisation.

(iii)   Linked to the above point is the fact that freedom to spend could make it difficult to implement the key policies and plans of the organisation. This could mean that unit managers in a hospital might generate expenditure on hospitals while the thrust of the authority's policies was to promote community care.

(iv)   A lack of detailed content of budgets at the beginning of a financial year means that budgetary control becomes that much more difficult to implement. Identifying reasons for under- and over-spendings and taking effective corrective action become more difficult as budgets have only been prepared as single total amounts.

(b)   Four examples of ways in which budget holders can be given flexibility in the management of their budgets are as follows.

(i)   Provisions can be created to allow underspendings on revenue account to be carried forward into the following financial year. This system avoids budget holders spending unnecessarily at the end of one financial year in case the underspendings are seen as being the result of too high a budget being set. It also means that balances can be built up to finance a special item of equipment or perhaps an attendance at a training course, etc.

(ii)   Virement is frequently used to allow flexibility. This is where funds which are seen as not required on one budget heading are transferred to finance increased expenditure on a separate budget heading. This mechanism has to be controlled and the transfer authorised prior to the expenditure being incurred. Thus surplus funds on a printing and stationery budget might be used to finance newly identified needs on the training budget.

(iii)   Budget holders can apply for extra resources during the year via a system of supplementary estimates, eg, to meet unforeseen and essential demand for a service such as radiology or pathology. Again prior approval of the expenditure is required and the resources are usually released from the central reserves of the organisation, etc.

(iv)   Unforeseen expenditure or expenditure increases over and above an estimated amount are usually financed from a contingency provision. Thus actual pay awards are frequently in excess of estimated pay awards, the difference being financed out of a central fund or contingency set up specifically to finance such expenditure. Similarly, totally unplanned expenditure, eg, damage caused by floods and gales, can be financed via the central contingency.

3.30   INVESTMENT APPRAISAL

(a)   **Payback period**

		Project X	**Project Y**
Initial outlay		£150,000	£250,000
Return year	1	50,000	25,000
	2	50,000	25,000
	3	50,000	25,000
	4	–	25,000
	5	–	50,000
	6	–	100,000
Therefore payback period		3 years	6 years

Average annual rate of return on average capital employed

	Project X	Project Y
Average capital employed	$\dfrac{150,000}{2}$	$\dfrac{250,000}{2}$
	= £75,000 $\checkmark$	= £125,000 $\checkmark$
Average return	$\dfrac{187,500}{4}$	$\dfrac{525,000}{8}$
	= £46,875	= £65,625
∴ Return	62.5%	52.5%

In both cases Project X is ranked above Project Y.

(b) Payback has the advantage of being easy to calculate and simple to understand. Its time horizons are relatively short and perhaps because of this its results are more accurate and less susceptible to poor forecasting. The projects preferred by this method mean that the company's liquidity is put at less risk as cash generated quickly is the principal criterion.

The return on capital employed is also simple to calculate and produces a percentage figure which is easy to understand and compare. It benefits from considering the whole life of a project rather than focussing on receipts up to the payback point. This is sensible as many large capital schemes do not yield positive returns in early years.

(c) The above two techniques ignore one significant factor, namely that money has a time value. It is undeniable that money received today has a greater value than money received or promised sometime in the future. This is not just due to the risk of default or the presence of inflation. Rather it is the fact that money received today can be invested or used to purchase goods. Discounted cash flow recognises this fact and discounts the receipts and payments to a common price base (ie, gives the money an exchange value). This is achieved by using a discount rate based on the cost of borrowing to finance the project.

Discounted cash flow uses two basic techniques. The first is the net present value method which calculates the difference between the discounted receipts and payments arising from a capital project. The preferred project is usually the one with the greatest positive present value. The second method, the internal rate of return method, establishes the discount rate giving a net present value of zero. This discount rate equates to the earnings produced by an investment.

3.31 FIVE PRINCIPLES

(a) The following five principles should form the basis of any central government grants to public sector organisations.

(i) Central government has been elected to manage the economy and therefore needs to control and influence the level of spending by public sector organisations in the light of centrally determined policies and priorities; this will be reflected in the level and distribution of any grant.

(ii) Any grant level calculation should be easy to understand, and the calculation should be on accepted bases, such as population size and the age structure of the population.

(iii) The grant should be easy to administer and the costs of administering and controlling grant payments should be kept to a minimum.

(iv) The level of grant should reduce the level of tax burden or charge paid by local people who use the services offered by the public sector organisation.

(v) The monitoring of grant spending by public sector organisations should identify extravagant or high spending organisations and thus control spending levels within the resources available.

(b) (i) The spending of nationalised industries is controlled by central government by the setting of an annual cash–limited external financial limit. A specific nationalised industry's external financing limit is the total of grants and net borrowings and is the amount of spending that the industry can undertake in a particular financial year.

The cash–limited external financing limit is determined annually after consultation with the financial managers of the industry, taking into account capital expenditure forecasts and the money available from internal sources.

(ii) The grant–related expenditure assessment was part of the complex calculation of an individual local authority's block grant before the introduction of the revenue support grant in 1990.

However, the revenue support grant is calculated in a much more straightforward manner.

– Calculate the assessed spending need (ASN) per adult at taxpayer level for all local authority areas.

– Identify the area with the lowest ASN per adult at taxpayer level.

– Calculate how much grant is needed in total to bring the needs of all areas down to the lowest need area.

– Allocate any grant remaining from the total amount available for revenue support grant as a flat rate amount per adult to all local authority areas.

(iii) The public expenditure survey system is the planning system by which the government reviews and plans the level of public expenditure for the next three years ahead in the light of the estimated funds available to finance that expenditure.

The system commences in April each year when the Cabinet agrees guidelines regarding the overall level of public expenditure in the light of the income available from taxation and borrowing. Ministers submit bids for money and these are discussed by the Cabinet. The Chancellor of the Exchequer makes an autumn statement which contains details of the government's public expenditure plans for the next three years. These details are then finalised by the Cabinet and a White Paper is produced which details the distribution and levels of public expenditure across the various government departments.

3.32 FINANCE DEPARTMENT

(a) Six key functions of the finance department in a local authority:

(i) **Revenue budgeting:** Finance department staff are involved in the annual revenue budgeting cycle. They are responsible for standardising the format of estimate submissions from committees and liaise with the appropriate spending department regarding the levels of spending. They compile the budget for the authority and ensure that the estimates it contains are in line with the council's agreed spending policies and priorities.

(ii) **Capital budgeting:** A capital programme will be compiled for the authority normally on the basis of a five year rolling cycle. It will contain detailed capital budgets of individual committees. Finance department staff will be involved in compiling these budgets, providing financial information to help determine priorities and ensuring that funds are available when the capital projects commence.

(iii) **Centralised accounting and financial information system:** One of the major functions of the finance department is to maintain the accounting records for all the service committees of the authority. The accounting system will provide regular budgetary control statements to managers to enable them to monitor income and expenditure levels and compare these with the estimated levels. Normally income and expenditure is coded to a cost centre to enable managers to control costs. The accounting system will also provide the information which forms the basis of the authority's annual financial statements.

(iv) **Financial advice:** Finance department staff will provide financial advice to councillors and officers throughout the authority. They will advise on such things as the financial implications of government directives and guidelines, and the cost of alternative policy decisions.

(v) **Cash collection:** The cashiers section of the finance department acts as the centralised collection point for the authority. Facilities will be available for electors of the area to pay their rates/community charge in cash as well as the payment for other services such as housing. The income section will be responsible for coordinating and monitoring the cash collection procedures and collecting income through the issue of accounts. This income will be received by post or by direct payment into the authority's bank account.

(vi) **Internal audit:** The internal audit section is located in the finance department and will carry out its functions in line with the CIPFA Role and Responsibilities Statement:

'Internal audit is an independent appraisal function within an organisation for the review of activities as a service to all levels of management. It is a control which measures, evaluates and reports upon the effectiveness of internal controls, financial and others as a contribution to the efficient use of resources within an organisation.'

(b) Three areas of work which a chief financial officer is unlikely to delegate on a regular basis to one of his/her staff are:

(i)   Personal attendance at major committees and council, because as the 'responsible financial officer' appointed under Section 151 of the Local Government Act 1972 he/she is ultimately responsible for the financial affairs of the authority.

(ii)   Attendance at management team meetings, as the responsible financial officer and a key member of the top management of the authority. Attendance ensures contact with other chief officers and the ability to influence the policy–making process.

(iii)   Interviewing for key senior posts in the finance department. As chief financial officer he/she is responsible for recruiting high calibre and efficient qualified staff.

3.33   INTERNAL AUDIT

(a)   Five points which are likely to be included in financial regulations governing the operation of internal audit in a local authority are as follows.

(i)   Naming of the chief financial officer as the responsible financial officer appointed under Section 151 of the Local Government Act 1972 and as such responsible for maintaining an adequate and effective internal audit of the accounts of the body;

(ii)   reference to the delegation of the responsibility detailed above to the internal auditors employed by the authority;

(iii)   confirmation that internal auditors in carrying out the duties delegated to them by the chief financial officer have a right of access at reasonable times to all financial records and supporting information;

(iv)   confirmation that internal auditors have the right to ask employees of the authority for information and explanation while carrying out their duties;

(v)   the detailed procedures to be followed when fraud is suspected or discovered; this will involve reporting the matters to the chief financial officer, with the chief internal auditor being named as the individual delegated to investigate the suspicion or fraud.

(b)   The CIPFA 'Role and objectives statement' defines internal audit as follows:

'Internal audit is an independent appraisal function within an organisation for the review of activities as a service to all levels of management. It is a management control which measures, evaluates and reports upon the effectiveness of internal control and the efficient use of resources within an organisation.'

Internal check is best regarded as those checks on the day–to–day transactions which operate continuously as part of the routine system, whereby the work of one person is proved independently of, or is complementary to, the work of another, the object being the prevention or early detection of errors and fraud.

Internal check therefore includes such matters as the allocation of authority, the division of work, the proper method of recording transactions and the use of independently ascertained totals against which a large number of individual entries can be proved such as a purchases/creditors ledger control account.

The contrast between the function of internal audit and the operation of internal check can be illustrated as follows.

A purchases system will incorporate various internal checks such as that when an order is placed it is made on an approved serially numbered order and that all orders are authorised by a responsible officer. When the goods are received one individual signs the invoice to state the goods are received. Another person will check the arithmetical accuracy of the order and a designated responsible officer will authorise the invoice for payment. This division of duties forms part of the system of internal check.

Internal audit's responsibility is to monitor and review the system to ensure that the procedures are operating effectively to prevent error and fraud.

3.34   FINANCING EXPENDITURE

(a)   An alternative way of acquiring the benefits of a capital asset such as machinery, vehicles, and buildings is to lease the asset. Under this method the asset belongs to the leasing company and is used by the public authority in return for an annual lease rental.

Four advantages of leasing

(i)   Leasing is flexible – the lessee generally has the choice of supplier of equipment, and the terms of the lease are generally tailored to the requirements of the lessee.

(ii)   Development grants and capital allowances may be claimed by the lessor and these are passed on in the form of reduced rental payments, making leasing a cheap form of finance.

(iii)   Leasing is a readily available source of short/medium term finance.

(iv)   Leasing allows a 'fair' charge to the revenue accounts since the asset is paid for over its useful life – equitable to the rate payers.

Four disadvantages

(i)   The authority is legally tied to leasing the equipment for a minimum period of time.

(ii)   Leasing funds may not always be available in the future as central government may intervene in leasing with regard to capital allowances. These allowances are what make leasing houses' terms so attractive to public authorities.

(iii)   Leasing houses tend to limit their agreements to three- to seven–year periods and hence authorities may find that leasing funds are not available to finance longer term capital expenditure.

(iv)   Central government controls can restrict the use of leasing as a way of financing capital expenditure. Such controls reduce the ability of public authorities to supplement their annual capital expenditure allocations by entering into leasing agreements.

(b)   Temporary loans as a form of borrowing became increasingly significant in the 1950s and early 1960s. High interest rates persuaded local authorities to defer issuing longer term securities in the hope that rates would fall, so enabling the longer term loan to be obtained more cheaply.

The loans are generally raised through a money broker who is paid commission for setting up the loan. The only acknowledgement is usually a simple deposit receipt with the terms and conditions of the loan written on it. Interest can be adjusted by notice on either side according to the period for which the loan is made (eg, two days, seven days, etc).

Four advantages of temporary borrowing

(i) It is generally cheaper than long–term borrowing because of lower interest rates.

(ii) It is a flexible method because borrowings can be related to cash flows and thus kept to a minimum.

(iii) It can be used when a drop in long–term interest rates is expected in the future and thus the authority can borrow now and fund later when rates are lower.

(iv) The temporary money market presents an essential lending market for authorities with temporary surplus funds.

Four disadvantages of temporary borrowing

(i) The authority may be given notice to repay large amounts of temporary borrowings which may be very difficult and very costly to replace.

(ii) The short–term interest rates are very volatile and much more affected by the money supply on the day than are rates for long–term borrowings.

(iii) The administration costs of negotiating and settling loans on a regular basis are higher than those associated with long–term loans, and a specialist loans officer is normally employed.

(iv) Temporary borrowing levels and the use of money raised are frequently subject to changes in statutory restrictions and there is a constant need for the loans officer to keep up to date and advise the Treasurer accordingly.

3.35   PAY

(a) Cash management is improved. Cash remains in the organisation longer as staff are paid 12 times per year as opposed to 52 times per annum. This better cashflow could be reflected in lower interest charges and greater interest earned.

Secondly, savings in payroll preparation costs such as computer time, staff number and stationery costs could accrue to the organisation.

Finally, lower security costs and associated insurance premiums should be seen as a result of having less cash moving around the system.

(b) Employees will need encouragement to change payment procedures. These could include:

(i) involvement of trade unions and employees in all aspects of the change;

(ii)   provision of banking facilities to cash cheques and provide bank services on public sector premises;

(iii) cash incentives to move from weekly to monthly pay, eg, offering to pay bank charges for two years;

(iv)   providing a loan to employees to ease the period of change from weekly to monthly pay.

(c)   Benefits of a bank account include the following.

(i)   Greater security for the assets of employees as they no longer have to carry large amounts of cash around on pay day.

(ii)   Bank account holders find it easier to obtain the other facilities offered by banks such as personal loans and overdraft facilities; preferential treatment is often received by account holders.

(iii) It allows the employee to manage and plan cash uses more easily. For example regular bank statements are available, paid cheques act as proof of payment and budget accounts are available at most banks.

(iv)   Standing orders and direct debit facilities are an easy way to pay bills. There is no need to remember to pay bills since these are arranged automatically by the bank, thereby increasing the employees' leisure time.

(v)   Savings accounts can be opened which encourage saving on a regular basis and do not leave saving to chance or the whim of the employee.

3.36   OBJECTIVES

(a)   Setting objectives assists the planning process in the following ways.

(i)   Setting objectives facilitates both the agreement of priorities and when they should be implemented. The objectives act as a benchmark against which to judge competing claims and their relative urgency. Choices are made easier to justify to the electorate and the local taxpayer.

(ii)   Once objectives are set say by a local authority council, then the officers of the council have a framework within which to operate. Targets can be set for individual managers and departments thus fostering a corporate approach to the implementation of plans.

(iii) Objectives can be reflected in individual standards of performance which can form the basis of monitoring actual performance. Targets could be set in terms of crimes committed to reflect an objective of reducing the number of burglaries in urban areas. The standards encourage accountability and responsibility on the part of both officers and members.

(iv)   Objectives allow elected and appointed members to define clearly the purpose of any public sector body. The electorate can make their judgement via the ballot box. Defined objectives allow consumers and/or electors to support or reject a particular course of action.

(b) Internal audit objectives include:

   (i) an essential cornerstone of management control: namely, reviewing and reporting on systems, procedures, objectives, planning process, etc; in other words, a means of monitoring value for money;

   (ii) appraising, implementing and monitoring systems of internal control and internal check in the organisation;

   (iii) an independent review system in ad hoc areas, such as systems audit, performance measurement and security arrangements, etc – this often involves a management–consulting role.

(c) Chief financial officers can and should provide advice to the objective setters. This advice should be unbiased, professional and independent: the financial resources available, the financial consequences of objectives, the statutory backing of expenditure, the overall budget and/or community charge impact of the objectives. Financial advice must be available at the most appropriate place in the planning process. This advice can often temper the enthusiasm and optimism of politicians and other professionals.

3.37 CAPITAL PROGRAMMES AND BUDGETS

(a) Capital budgets allow public sector organisations to comply with central government controls. For example, by forecasting the cost and timing of capital projects, local authorities can more easily remain with their annual basic credit approval in respect of capital expenditure.

Capital budgets allow the revenue consequences of capital projects to be quantified. This not only facilitates planning but also allows the impact on charges and/or poll tax levels to be identified. The revenue conseqeuences will include the running expenses such as salaries and wages plus the cost of borrowing to finance the project.

Bringing together capital projects in a capital budget covering several years allows the financial and non–financial aspects to be more easily co–ordinated. Priorities and plans are clearly identified in the capital budget.

Like all budgets, the capital budget can be used as an instrument of control by monitoring actual costs and progress against budgeted costs and progress. The budget allows problems of implementation to be identified and corrected more quickly.

(b) The way in which the project is to be financed: for example, is the computer to be purchased via a loan or leased? This is particularly important for local authorities having to stay within an aggregate credit limit.

The total capital cost needs to be available and this should be detailed over the key expenditure headings such as land, building work and furniture. This is necessary to allow those making decisions to assess the total financial impact and make some judgement about value for money.

Revenue consequences need to be available to allow decision–makers to assess whether the authority will have sufficient resources to operate the capital project: for example, will the hospital be able to fund the running costs of a new ward from existing resources or will economies or expenditure cuts be necessary?

(c) Variation orders occur when the original specifications of a tender are changed; for example, a different type of brickwork or insulation material may be requested as a police station is being built. This variation should be agreed by the policy authority before the work is carried out, with the technical specifications and cost being itemised in the variation order.

An amount included in a tender for a capital project to cover the estimated cost of works which cannot be easily forecast in advance is a provisional sum. The actual cost of the sum is paid to the contractor and replaces the provisional estimate included in the original tender. This could cover the cost of building foundations which are greatly influenced by the type and quality of the soil structure.

As capital projects can take several months or years to complete, contractors require payments on account as the work proceeds. These payments are authorised by the quantity surveyor issuing an interim certificate. The certificates are agreed by measuring and valuing the work completed to date. The certificates are authorised and audited before the cheque is issued.

3.38 INSURANCE TERMS AND INSURANCE FUNDS

(a) Claims made by employees against their employer are covered by employer's liability insurance. If an employee is injured whilst performing his/her job and the employer is shown to be legally liable for such injury, then compensation would be claimed by the employee. This type of insurance reflects the legal duty of employers to provide safe working conditions.

A loss of cash or other tangible assets incurred by an organisation as a result of the dishonesty of its employees is covered by fidelity guarantee insurance. Such policies can either identify specific staff or be blanket policies covering all employees of the organisation. Similarly the policy can include losses incurred as a result of employees not carrying out their duties in a safe manner; for example, a cashier not locking a safe or not banking receipts promptly.

Good faith is a principle underlying all insurance agreements. This places responsibilities on both the insured and the insurer. The latter must clearly specify the terms and limitations of the insurer's liability. The insured has a duty to reveal all material information relating to the insured risk, such as a significant increase in the monetary value of the risk.

To encourage organisations to ensure risks are insured at an appropriate value, the average clause usually applies. If a building is damaged by fire but it is found that the value insured is significantly less then the value of the building, then the insurer is only liable to pay a proportion of the replacement cost. This proportion is assessed by relating the insured sum to the value of property.

(b) An alternative to insuring risks via private insurance companies is to set up an insurance fund. This is an internal fund which will meet the cost of insurance claims for identified low risks.

It involves the authority making annual payments equivalent to those which would have been paid as premiums to outside insurance companies. The premiums paid into the fund are available to meet insurance claims and any surplus fund balances can be invested to generate interest to increase the size of the fund.

(c) An insurance fund can reduce the costs of insurance mainly because the profit included in private insurance company premiums is not paid by the authority.

Secondly, the cash paid out to external insurance companies is paid into the fund. These monies are available to the authority and can be invested to earn interest for the fund. These interest receipts swell the size of the fund and are available to meet insurance claims.

However, it is possible for the fund balance to be insufficient to meet particular claims, particularly in the early years of establishing the fund. This disadvantage can be minimised by restricting claims to low risk insurance.

Setting up and maintaining an insurance fund is expensive and certainly it is difficult to match the economies of scale available to large private insurance companies.

3.39 STAFFING LEVELS AND BONUS SCHEMES

(a) Encouraging staff to retire early is advantageous because it allows employees to choose their own future. It can also reduce costs more rapidly as the staff who leave are usually older people on higher salaries. Of course, early retirement has financial costs which can include expensive lump sum payments or making up pension rights. Early retirement might be taken by experienced staff which could result in problems in maintaining the quality of service with less experienced staff.

An alternative to early retirement is compulsory redundancy where the staff to leave are selected by the management. Obviously it allows management more freedom to identify which staff should leave. However, it can create industrial relations problems by raising opposition from trades unions and employees. It is also necessary to negotiate attractive redundancy terms which might be both expensive to implement and time-consuming to negotiate. Advantages can accrue to management if terms are favourable as industrial disputes can be minimised and costs reduced as staff accept the terms quickly.

Finally the non-filling of vacancies as a result of staff leaving of their own volition is a way of reducing payroll costs. The vacant posts (arising as a result of retirement or people leaving) are not filled and duties are redeployed over the remaining staff. It is a relatively cheap method as no extra redundancy costs are involved and also industrial disputes are unlikely as the staff are leaving by choice not compulsion. It is, however, a slow method of reducing costs and can leave essential posts unfilled. Similarly the redeployment of the duties associated with the vacant post is likely to produce resentment and will probably affect the efficiency of remaining staff.

(b) Bonus schemes have the following drawbacks:

(i) the scheme can encourage employees to reduce the quality of their work in order to increase the quantity of work and thus maximise bonus payments;

(ii) bonus schemes complicate payroll preparation and calculation and this can result in increased costs associated with administering and controlling the bonus scheme;

(iii) internal controls verifying bonus payments can increase staff numbers and reduce productivity;

(iv) employees may take risks with safety procedures in order to maximise bonus payments – this can result in compensation claims, breakdowns in provision of goods or services and of course poorer quality products.

The advantages include:

(i) bonus schemes, if properly devised, can encourage employees to maximise productivity without the need for detailed supervision – this not only reduces costs but can improve employee motivation;

(ii) the unit costs of the product or service can be reduced as the increased productivity spreads the fixed costs over more units of service – these reductions can be reflected in pricing policies;

(iii) bonus schemes, if implemented with the involvement of unions and employees, can improve the morale and motivation of the workforce – the employees have more control of their working conditions and also their level of pay.

3.40 RECENT LEGISLATION

(a) (i) Discretionary expenditure

Prior to the 1989 Act, discretionary expenditure had been controlled under Section 137 of the Local Government Act 1972. The principal feature of this control centred on the fact that a local authority could only incur expenditure which in their opinion was in the interests of their area (eg, promoting economic development). The expenditure under Section 137 in any one financial year could not exceed the product of a 2p rate.

Following the Widdecombe report in 1986, which reported into the conduct of local authority business, it was suggested that the government should consult with local authorities and draw up a set of guidelines that would clarify the legitimate use to which the 2p rate could be put. The reason for this was that the government was concerned that some local authorities were using the funding to promote political campaigns and circumvent government controls. Widdecombe suggested that any discretionary expenditure should be 'easy to understand, predictable and equitable as between one area and other'.

The 1989 Act (Sections 36–38) amends previous legislation and takes on board much of the Widdecombe recommendations. Local authorities can incur expenditure which in their opinion is in the interests of, and will bring direct benefit to, their area. This direct benefit must be identifiable to specific groups of people.

The new legislation is much more specific than previously and the maximum amount expendable in a year is such that county councils and non–metropolitan districts multiply their defined population by £2.50, metropolitan districts and London boroughs by £5, and parish or community councils by £3.50.

(ii) **Definition of capital expenditure**

The 1989 Act replaced that contained in the Planning and Land Act 1980. Section 40 of the 1989 Act is more specific and precise. Capital expenditure relates to the following tangible assets:

- the acquisition, reclamation, enhancement or laying out of land, exclusive of roads, buildings and other structures;

- the acquisition, construction preparation, enhancement or replacement of roads, buildings or other structures;

- the acquisition, installation or replacement of moveable or immovable plant, machinery and apparatus and vehicles and vessels;

- the making of advances or grants or other financial assistance to any person towards expenditure incurred on any of the above categories;

- the acquisition of share capital or loan capital in any body corporate insofar as it is not expenditure on improved investments.

The Secretary of State may direct any expenditure he sees fit as being capital for capital purposes.

(iii) **Borrowing and borrowing limits**

The underpinning part of the 1989 Act is Part IV which states that all expenditure must be treated as revenue expenditure in the year it is incurred, unless it is for capital purposes as described in (ii) above.

(b) The Planning and Land Act 1980 was previously the controlling legislation for capital spending. It centred its controls on the principle of annual spending ceilings termed 'capital expenditure allocation blocks'. These prescribed the maximum annual payments that could be made on schemes falling within the definition of capital expenditure. The source of funding was not restricted and any payments made against the blocks automatically qualified for loan sanction.

The new system shifts its control principles from that of controlling expenditure to that of controlling the source of funding, namely borrowing or that which has the same economic effect as borrowing. Under the new system each authority receives an aggregate credit limit (ACL) to which it must work. The ACL includes the authority's temporary revenue and capital borrowing ceilings, the authority's credit ceiling plus the difference between their approved investments/cash and their usable capital receipts.

For each financial year an authority will receive a basic credit approval which is equal to the annual capital guideline less any receipts taken into account.

Capital charges will now comprise of two components:

(i) depreciation calculated on normal commercial accounting principles but based on the average current replacement cost of the authority's assets;

(ii)   interest calculated on the current replacement cost of the authority's capital assets (6% being the Treasury's test discount figure).

Objectives

(i)   To increase the awareness of health service managers of the costs of capital.

(ii)   To provide incentives to use capital efficiently.

(iii) To ensure that capital charges are fully reflected in the pricing of hospital services, in order to promote fair competition within the NHS and with the private sector.

3.41   TAXALL DISTRICT COUNCIL

Date:

Reference:

Dear Mrs Grant

Community Charge Bill 19X0/X1

Thank you for your recent letter regarding the above. May I take this opportunity to welcome your comments and hopefully to explain some complexities of the new system and thereby answer the points you have raised.

As you already know, the community charge was introduced on 1 April 1990 and replaced the rating system. The new tax is a flat-rate tax on basically all adults in the local authority area. This means there are considerably more people paying the new local tax.

To deal with some of your specific points, I would like to respond as follows.

Your net community charge of £356.80 represents the maximum amount due from you after allowing for income received from central government and business property. I say the maximum amount due as people on low incomes are entitled to rebates or community charge benefit of up to 80% to help pay the tax. I have enclosed a leaflet giving details on rebates and on how to apply. If you think that you may qualify it is important that you should do so immediately. These rebates are paid for largely by the government.

Taxall District Council is the authority which has the job of collecting community charges on behalf of itself and other authorities in your area, namely Bakershire County Council and Thatcham Parish Council. The word 'precept' represents the amount which has to be collected to pay for the services provided by local authorities. Taxall District Council collects the tax and pays the relevant amounts over to the respective local authorities; in this area the total required is £866.90 per head of population.

The community charge receipts when collected are paid into a collection fund which is a statutory account maintained by Taxall District Council. This fund also records all the payments made to the respective local authorities out of monies collected and other items such as those relating to national non-domestic rates (the business rate) and the revenue support grant received from the government.

There are two deductions shown on your bill, namely the business rate and the revenue support grant. The latter is an amount contributed by central government from general taxation towards the cost of providing local services. In 1990/91 it represents about 25% of the total expenditure in this area. The business rates are those charged on properties other than domestic property. The business rate poundage is set annually by central government and is the same for all non-domestic ratepayers. The business rates are paid into a central pool managed by the Department of the Environment and Taxall District Council receives from the pool a sum proportional to the number of community charge-payers in its area.

Your final point relates to the SSA of £278. Under the new system if each local authority spends at a level equivalent to its standard spending assessment (SSA), local charge-payers will pay an identical community charge of £278. The SSA is central government's view of the cost to each authority of providing a standard level of service. It should be noted that these are central government's assessment for the purposes of sharing out central government grant and provide a comparative figure against which the charge-payers can judge spending in their area. Local authorities are free to provide a different level of service and obviously may vary in their efficiency. The £78.80 will therefore not be refunded but is spent on services which the elected members deem to be necessary or desirable to the residents of this area.

The community charge is a complex subject and like anything new takes some time to understand. I trust the above explanations shed some light on the topic. Should you require further explanations please do not hestitate in contacting me.

Yours sincerely

3.42 DEVHAM COUNTY

(a) Any statistical comparison must be treated with caution as we may not be comparing like with like. The county areas are very different in characteristics in both geographical terms as well as population mix, structure and distribution.

The statistics are very selective in their content in the sense that the net expenditure is not fully analysed; it is unclear what is contained in the figures and what has been omitted.

Averages are very dangerous statistical tools because here we are not clear whether we are dealing with an arithmetic mean and indeed whether the median/mode might be more useful.

(b) A more meaningful comparison of financial information may be made if more care is taken in selecting the authorities and establishments used as comparators to make sure they are of the same type. Rather than use an average of all counties it would be more realistic to use an average for all authorities/establishments of the same type. Comparisons will small numbers of authorities or clusters, chosen because they have more in common with Devham, are better. The development of clusters of similar authorities by reference to social and economic data such as age, structure, household size, family characteristics, occupations, unemployment, cost of living, etc, would be useful. This use of clusters however can suffer if one authority is very different from the others in the cluster distorting the average.

(c) Efficiency is primarily concerned with the relationship between input of expenditure and output of product or service; it thus attempts to measure the relationship between the level of service provided and the resources used in achieving such a level of service.

Effectiveness is concerned with achieving objectives. Has the desired result been achieved by the outputs?

These are both important concepts particularly in the public sector because they are a means of assessing changes in the level and impact of a service over time. The measurement of efficiency and effectiveness provide customers, policy makers and officers with information so they are better placed to exercise choice and decide about service quality. They are a means of monitoring and controlling progress against plans; of justifying the use of resources; providing a basis for calculating incentives and rewards; and are a major part of assessing whether value for money is being obtained.

Examples of efficiency measures in the Leisure and Recreation area might include price per meal as used in the statistics, cost per theatre seat, cost per booking, ratio of leisure centre income to expenditure, cost per tourist contact, cost per 1,000 population, number of swimmers per hour per assistant at leisure centres, etc.

Examples of effectiveness might include percentage of users that rate the service as satisfactory (eg, in terms of opening hours/choice/accessibility of services); percentage of children taught to swim; usage of facilities by targeted groups (eg, the unemployed, ethnic minorities); number and rate of catchment area residents using the service.

(c) Public sector organisations like any other are keen to demonstrate that they are economic, efficient and effective in their activities. They are especially keen to do so because of statutory responsibility and because of best serving the public interest in utilising public money. However, it is relatively easy to deal with aspects of economy because of its quantifiable and therefore objective nature. Efficiency and effectiveness are a little more difficult to measure and thus objectively assess.

3.43 BUDGETARY CONTROL

(a) It is important that the colleague concerned appreciates the rationale behind the proposals namely:

That the budget process is a financial expression of policy. It thus follows that the closer this process can get to those that are responsible for delivering and executing that policy, the better. Devolving budget preparation and budgetary control to service deliverers will mean that the whole process will be more appropriate and hence responsive to need and thus fulfils the following general objectives:

(i) preparing a budget reflecting the type and level of service determined by the policy makers;

(ii) a means of assessing the effectiveness of managers, in financial terms, in implementing their responsibilities;

(iii) a means of monitoring performance throughout the year;

(iv) a means of identifying areas of performance which require corrective action; and

(v)   a means of motivating managers' contribution towards the achievement of the organisation's goals.

(b)   There are of course reasons why your colleague could be afraid of such changes to the budget process. These could include:

(i)   a lack of knowledge and understanding of financial procedures and terminology;

(ii)   poor training and explanation as to the purpose of the changes to the budget process and of the colleague's role within the process;

(iii)   unclear definition by management of the colleague's responsibilities and authority when preparing and managing a budget;

(iv)   limited participation within the budget preparation process by the budget holder;

(v)   setting unattainable standards or targets for budget holders when viewed against available resources;

(vi)   inadequate detail, content and timing of budgetary control statements or lack of training or access to on–line computer budget information systems;

(vii)   lack of explanation of the linkage between the financial figures and the colleague's professional duties; and

(viii)   an overemphasis on the control aspects of budgets at the expense of plans, objectives and quality of service.

(c)   Ways of reducing the above fears include the following.

(i)   More participation is needed in the setting of budgets by those responsible for achieving budgets. This has been shown to be a motivating factor in achieving budget targets. Greater participation in the budget process increases motivation by encouraging responsibility and gives the budget holder a sense of ownership.

(ii)   Aspiration levels/expectation targets should be considered in setting budgets. Producing budgets which are almost impossible to achieve (ie, well above aspiration level of the budget holder) is unlikely to motivate an individual to achieve good performance.

(iii)   There should be adequate training of staff in the aims and purposes of the new budget process so that they see their role and responsibilities in relation to the organisation as a whole.

(iv)   Ensure there is a regular communication and support between budget holders and a nominated accountant. This supportive role is particularly important in the early stages of the change.

(v)   Uncontrollable and controllable costs should be clearly distinguished (ie, costs which the budget holder cannot control may be best segregated and not charged to those who cannot control them). Although to include them gives the service manager a better understanding of the 'total cost' of providing a service.

(vi) Where a budget holder achieves their budget or a favourable variance it could be acknowledged as a success. Similarly an adverse variance may not reflect the budget holder as a failure. In both cases other factors should be considered (eg, original budget level, inflation, external influences) and be used to determine what action should be taken to improve future performance.

(vii) Improved computer facilities and access together with the appropriate training.

Overall the aim is to create an environment in which budgets are viewed as facilitating rather than constraining or restraining.

3.44 BUDGET STATEMENT

(a) The statement is of a very limited nature in both content and format. It does not supply basic information appropriate to managerial need. The following would be an improvement.

(i) A clear indication of whether the budget is under or over spent by the use of =/– symbols. Equally the symbols could be used to signify degree of variance and could be used as advance warning.

(ii) The statement assumes all expenditure is similar and has a uniform cashflow. Salaries are not the same as wages. Salaries may be fairly stable and can be divided into twelve equal instalments; wages cannot. Also on a more general front there may well be seasonal fluctuations in expenditure patterns, therefore, the provisions figure must be analysed in more detail.

(iii) There needs to be a more detailed breakdown of the month being considered as well as the cumulative figures.

(iv) There needs to be an inclusion of budgeted and actual staff numbers expressed as whole time equivalents.

(b) The salaries and wages budget is underspent which could be explained by:

(i) staff vacancies;

(ii) staff on lower points of scale than provided for in budget;

(iii) inflation/annual pay awards less than budget provision;

(iv) mix and grades of staff different from original agreed budget;

(vi) reduction in overtime payments, etc, due to changes in rotas/working practices;

(vii) lower demand for the service requiring less staffing.

The provisions budget has an adverse variance which might be explained by:

(i) lack of control in requisitioning stocks;

(ii) level of stock at start and end of period;

(iii) price increases in excess of those budgeted for;

(iv) increases in the level of activity (eg, more use of catering department);

(v) phasing of budgets incorrect (eg, does not allow for seasonal variations);

(vi) wastage.

(c) Virement is the transfer of an underspent budget on one head to finance additional spending on another budget head; it can also be the transfer of unplanned income to finance additional spending.

A supplementary estimate is an approved increase to a budget head during a year sometimes financed from a contingency provision.

The application of both is regulated by a public sector organisation's financial regulations. As regards virement there are usually limits expressed in monetary terms which require different procedures. For example, transfers up to say £500 might only require the signature of both budget holders whereas, amounts above that might also have to be signed by a more senior officer or committee. There needs to be agreement as to the budget centres involved, the expense/income codes for both sides of the virement and the reasons for the transfer. There are also likely to be regulations which restrict virement when it is likely to generate recurrent expenditure in future years (eg, the appointment of staff).

A supplementary estimate could be regulated depending on its size, by either a senior officer and/or a committee. The expenditure should be necessary either for entirely new items or additional expenditure for which the original budget amount is inadequate. None of the expenditure should be incurred before the approval to the supplementary estimate is received.

(d) The key issue here is that whilst the costs have dropped by 10% the activity has dropped by 20%. Thus it is difficult to make a definite judgement without flexing the budget to reflect the actual activity achieved. Thus if all the budgeted costs were variable (ie, each x-ray should cost approximately £1.33) then the 12,000 produced should have cost £15,960 not the £18,000 incurred. On the other hand if the original budget has been entirely made up of fixed costs then a saving of £2,000 has been achieved. The question highlights the danger of comparing actual expenditure to a fixed rather than a flexed budget.

3.45 CAPITAL EXPENDITURE

(a) Six factors to be taken into account

(i) **Government and legal controls** – Local government can only do that which they have powers to do, anything else is 'ultra vires'.

(ii) **The effect of the method** chosen on current and future local taxpayers.

(iii) **Availability** of the chosen method. There is little point opting to borrow from the PWLB if the funds are not available or there is a statutory limiting factor.

(iv) **Timing** is also a crucial factor. A debt rescheduling package will take a long period of time to negotiate, there may not be such time available and therefore some other form of financing must be sought.

(v) **Cost** of chosen method. Borrowing versus using cash, and thus consideration of the level of interest rates both now and in the future.

(vi) **Appropriateness** and in the best interests of the public in the sense of probity and stewardship of public money. Therefore consideration must be given to both costs and benefits.

(b) (i) Capital budgets assist the co–ordination and planning of competing and/or complimentary projects.

(ii) To forecast the cashflows arising from a project to assist cash planning and borrowing policy.

(iii) To assess the revenue consequences of the capital project.

(iv) To monitor and control the progress and implementation of capital projects (eg, by use of critical path analysis to identify key dates).

(v) To assist in meeting the requirements of central government (eg, borrowing controls, expenditure plans, cash limits).

(vi) To co–ordinate the various methods of financing capital expenditure (eg, obtain better leasing terms or cheaper borrowing rates).

(c) Cost benefit analysis is a technique of investment appraisal; the appraisal is made in terms of the net social benefits accruing from the investment. It is necessary to identify the financial costs and revenues not only of the tangible benefits but also intangible benefits such as noise reduction, safety travel, secure environment, etc. Similarly it is necessary to identify intangible costs such as pollution, heavier traffic flows, reduction in property values, etc. Quantification is difficult and subjective particularly in respect of these tangible costs and benefits. Surrogate prices can be established by finding out what consumers would be willing to pay if there were a market in the intangible cost or benefit.

When all the benefits and costs have been quantified they are usually discounted to a present value; often an allowance is made for risk and uncertainty. In some instances only the tangible costs and benefits are quantified but a list is made of the other non–tangible costs and benefits to assist the decision–makers.

4 FINANCIAL PROCEDURES

4.1 PETTY CASH

(a) All public sector organisations and often individual departments within those organisations, hold petty cash. Petty cash is required to meet small often unexpected demands for expenditure such as stationery items, postage stamps, etc. Petty cash and payment by petty cash involve no official orders, receipt of invoices, etc. An employee may be given cash with which to make a purchase, or may pay his own money and claim reimbursement afterwards. He may be willing to do the latter if he knows he will be able to obtain cash immediately on return to the office.

(b) Petty cash is the responsibility of the chief financial officer and therefore it is his job to make sure records are kept accounting for the cash. In carrying out this function he should be aided by the financial regulations which will include some provisions for the handling of petty cash.

The responsibility for handling the cash should be delegated to one officer. The actual petty cash or cash float can then be given to the officer who must sign a receipt for it and then it can be placed in a safe. Access to the cash once there must be restricted to the officer responsible for it and then perhaps to one other senior officer and the internal auditor. The reason for restricting access to the petty cash in this way is one of security.

The petty cash can be drawn upon at any time and without notice to meet unexpected minor demands but before any is given, the person asking for the cash must produce a receipt which is authorised by a designated officer and then he must sign another receipt upon being given the cash.

Checks on the standing of the petty cash should be made fairly regularly and the cash held and payments made must be balanced. As the petty cash is used it will need to be reimbursed; the authorisation for reimbursement should come from the auditor or another senior officer. These reimbursements can be made using what is known as an 'imprest' system. The 'imprest' system involves the petty cash float being reimbursed at intervals to raise it to its original level. The imprest system works in the following way: first, each department or section requiring petty cash is given a lump sum which is expected to last for, say, a month. Limits on the nature and amount of petty cash payments are fixed. Claims for reimbursement must be fully supported by vouchers which must be authorised by a senior officer and then retained and cancelled by the officer in charge of the petty cash. A petty cash book should be kept, recording on the receipts side all sums received and on the payment side, an analysis of all sums paid out. At the end of the month all vouchers paid would be submitted, with a summary sheet showing expenditure codes to be debited to the finance department for reimbursement. At the end of the month a cheque would be received, covering the amount spent, and cashed at the bank, so bringing the imprest back to its original level. The internal auditor would verify the existence of authorised vouchers and unused cash from time to time.

Records of the petty cash need to be carefully maintained as the cash account forms part of the general ledger and is included in the final accounts. The petty cash is also subject to regular audits carried out by the internal auditor, whilst an external auditor will also check the petty cash account to see whether it balances.

4.2 CASHFLOW

(a)   The term 'cashflow' refers to the movement of cash into or out of various accounts. It therefore includes all types of payment, be this in cash, by cheque, bank credit, postal order, etc. The difference between the cash inflow and the cash outflow is the measurement of actual cashflow.

The inflow and outflow of cash is rarely in balance due to the different time-scales upon which payments and receipts operate. For example, some wages are paid weekly others monthly and receipt for work done or services provided also varies.

It is important to note also that there are differences between income and expenditure and their associated cash flows in the short-term, although these will equate in the long-term.

The management of cashflow is all inclusive, that is there is no separation or distinction between different funds, or between capital and revenue.

(b) Cashflow is important to a public sector organisation for a number of reasons. First, the services which the public sector organisation seeks to provide **need** the transfer of cash if they are to operate at all. Cash availability is all important in the operation of these services, and in order to ensure the future availability of cash it may often be necessary to take out short-term loans. If it is found that there is a cash surplus at any time then it is important not to let the money just sit; the extra cash can be invested and any temporary borrowing reduced.

The prerequisite for efficient control of cashflow is accurate forecasting of receipts. A system for forecasting and controlling receipts is as follows. First, assign the responsibility for cash control to a specific individual or team. Second, analyse the pattern of sales receipts over the last few months to establish the average delay period and how receipts typically flow in during the month. Third, use the receipts profile as a standard to control daily receipts during the current month.

In some cases the cashflow of a local authority may exceed its requirements due to its position as a taxing authority upon which others may precept. These precepts must be paid on the appointed dates, therefore cash must be available.

Cashflow is important, therefore, to a public sector organisation and it can yet be improved in a number of ways. A prompt collection of income will improve the cashflow of an organisation. To facilitate such a prompt collection the organisation can consider factoring and discounts, early billing, urgent recovery action and reduced credit periods. It must be noted, however, that the organisation will need to consider whether the disadvantages of such action in terms of deterring custom will outweigh the advantages gained in terms of improving cashflow.

Alongside the prompt collection of income, prompt banking will also improve the cashflow of a public sector organisation. Also, petty cash, stores and work in progress should be kept to an optimum minimum level and assets can be sold to raise cash.

The cash forecast is an integral part of managing the cashflow and indeed of efficient corporate financial planning. Management needs to forecast the cash position at a future date, say, in one year's time divided into monthly or even weekly intervals to find out how the money is coming in. More specifically, the purpose is to ensure that the organisation's working capital and cash are sufficient to carry out day-to-day transactions; also to indicate where surplus cash exists.

Finally, careful preparation and monitoring of the cash budget with daily updating and appropriate action where required will be of maximum benefit to an organisation.

4.3 CLEARING BANK SERVICES

(a) (i) A current account allows an organisation to pay its debts by means of a cheque which will be honoured by the bank by debiting funds from the current account of the organisation.

The organisation can pay money into the account by means of a paying-in slip accompanied by a cheque or cash. Other facilities provided include night safe facilities in which income can be deposited outside banking hours; also the organisation can pay in credits at any other branch of its particular bank and indeed at any other bank and it will be processed into the current account.

(ii) The bank will most often provide the organisation with an overdraft agreed upon by the bank manager and the finance officer of the organisation. An overdraft is very much a temporary loan which is resorted to when a longer-term loan is awaited, whilst waiting for other income, etc. The interest rate for an overdraft is fixed above the base rate and increases if the overdraft is not repaid within the specified limit. The granting of an overdraft and determination of its level is the responsibility of the bank's area office which takes into consideration the size and resources of the organisation.

(iii) The clearing bank can help an organisation in its payment of wages in a number of ways. It provides two major services, the Bank Automated Clearing Systems (BACS) and the Direct Bank Credit Transfers (DBC). These save the organisation charges for cheques and place the credit on the pay date.

An optimum cashflow position can be gained by BACS as the bank account of the organisation is debited on the same day as the employees' credits are made.

The bank also provides for the employees to cash their wage cheques and provides a facility to cash the total net wages cheque.

(iv) Computer magnetic tapes are tapes on which can be recorded the credit and debit **details** of an organisation which appear on a bank statement. The tapes, and all the information contained on them, can be fed directly from the bank's computer into the organisation's computer. This ensures prompt access to individual records and consequently allows for quick recovery action. It also saves expensive staff resources previously needed for manually listing, processing and balancing transactions.

(v) Direct telegraphic transfers provide for the debit and credit of accounts of both payer and payee on the same day. This means that payment can be made on the due date and an unnecessary balance need not be maintained in waiting for an unexpected transaction without being certain of the date it will be processed.

(b) (i) The reconciliation of a bank balance with a cash book balance requires the following procedure. First a date for reconciliation must be determined and then a request for a bank statement made as at the reconciliation date. The items need to be completed in the cash book and totalled also as at the reconciliation date. The next step involves a matching and comparison of items in the cash book and bank statement and then a listing of the non-matching items. The bank statement entries on the non-matching list need to be verified and then entered into the cash book whereupon the items in the cash book need to be retotalled and a balance obtained. The bank statement balance should then be adjusted for non-matching items. A final check should be made of both balances.

The following is a simple, numeric example.

Cash book

	£		
31.3.X4	50,300	Cr	Balance
	400	Dr	Bank interest/commission
	100	Dr	Dishonoured cheque
	200	Cr	Direct bank credit
	50,000		

Bank statement

	£		
31.3.X4	48,000	Cr	Balance
	4,000	Cr	Income not yet banked
	2,000	Dr	Unpresented cheques
	50,000		

4.4 ALLOCATION OF COSTS

(a) Central Administrative Expenses (CAE) is that part of an organisation's total expenditure which supports the direct provision of services but is not in the main identifiable with any one service.

The contribution of the CAE to the provision of a particular service is included in accounting the total costs of that service. The costs relating to CAE can be central support services, central departments, expenses relating to the board, the administrative buildings, etc. The full proportion of CAE should be borne by trading services, agency services, rechargeable works, to enable correct recharges and grant claims to be made and consequently enable a maximisation of income.

Central administrative expenses are allocated for a number of reasons. First, it is evident that the allocation of CAE provides for greater efficiency and expertise than if each service was totally self–supporting. Also financial control and accounting efficiency is available for each service through central administration.

It is extremely useful if CAE are treated uniformly by all organisations, for then this facilitates a better comparison of reports and statistics within and between organisations. Without this uniformity comparisons will be of far less worth. It is also important that there is an accurate allocation of CAE to ensure accurate costings especially in the light of the privatisation of some public sector organisations and the law relating to the rate of return of specific direct labour organisations. It must be noted, however, that there can never be a truly accurate allocation of CAE, they represent a **calculated** attempt to allocate central cost over services.

(b) Central administrative expenses may be allocated in a number of ways. For central support services the costs can be allocated on a usage basis, eg, telephones and extensions, photocopying on the number of copies produced, typing on the number of words or the time taken. The salaries and expenses of the central departments can be allocated according to the time spent on each service. This can be calculated either from detailed records or upon each officer's personal assessment.

The turnover for each service can be the basis for allocation of board or council expenses, although it can be noted in respect of certain functions that a basis of service related attendances may be more accurate. Service headings and departments are the basis for allocation of the running costs of the administrative buildings.

Generally standard service headings should be used to allocate CAE, these are normally prepared for the budget, the revised budget and for final outturn figures included in the organisation's final accounts.

4.5 CHANGING BANKERS

(a) The decision by an authority to change its banker should not be taken without thorough investigation because such a move can involve a great deal of financial and administrative disruption. The responsibility for the investigation lies with the chief financial officer; he, however, cannot authorise the change but must win the approval of the members.

The change in banker could be achieved by offering the authority's account for tender but a number of difficulties may be involved in using this procedure. First the lowest tender is not necessarily the one to be accepted as public authorities need certain facilities from a bank which the lowest tenderer may not be able to provide. Also there is difficulty even in establishing the lowest tender because the bases of charges vary considerably between banks. A third difficulty can often arise in the form of political pressure from members to change to a particular bank.

Once the actual change has taken place the authority will probably encounter a number of problems. To begin with the change will be inconvenient as it will undoubtedly confuse a number of debtors and ratepayers. Also in the early stages it will involve the parallel running of new and old bank accounts and consequently duplicated effort on the part of staff. The change will also involve increased costs in the short-term as cheques and stationery are reprinted and staff trained in the new banking facilities.

(b) The banks primarily use three methods of charging for facilities.

First, facilities are charged on a **flat rate**. This is a fixed amount for basic banking facilities and is paid over the year by the authority. Any extra facilities will be charged on an individual basis.

Second, the banks operate a **unit charge**. This is where the bank has a scale of charges for individual transactions, eg, cheques drawn. Often a charge is made for notional interest on credit balances on the authority's accounts. The weakness of this method lies in the fact that it takes no account of the value of the individual transactions and when an authority has a number of small value transactions it is bound to pay more.

A **turnover charge** is the third method of charging; it is based on aggregate withdrawals or aggregate turnover and therefore counters the weakness of the second method.

It can be said that no particular method of charging for facilities is better than another; each method needs to be assessed on the basis of estimated transactions. Generally the authorities negotiate charges with the bank through their chief financial officer and even then it is common practice for the authority to pay a commission charge for the maintenance of its account plus additional transaction charges for loan transactions or computer facilities.

4.6   CHECKING INVOICES

It is most important that invoices are checked both before and after they are paid by means of an internal check system.

A number of checks must be completed before invoices are passed to the chief financial officer for payment. First the internal check system needs to make sure that the organisation has actually received the goods, that they are the goods ordered and that they are in good condition. The system needs to check that the price charged is that which was agreed upon. It is important that the internal check system ensures that inventory items have been recorded, the invoice is arithmetically correct and there has been a cancellation of the copy order. Once all these checks have been made the officers responsible should certify this fact on the invoice, whilst a senior authorised officer divorced from these routine checks should make an overall certification for payment.

As far as 'certification' of the invoice is concerned, the 'authorised' officer's certification is evidence that all the requirements above have been carried out. There may be occasional difficulties as to who should certify certain classes of payment. The general rule is that 'authorised' officers should refrain from certifying an invoice for payment unless it is chargeable to an estimate head, which his department controls. This will avoid the danger of the same payment being originated in more than one department. The responsible officer's certification and coding details should then be entered on the gummed coding slip. Batches of certified invoices, duly certified should be forwarded to the Finance Department.

Due to the costs involved only a few invoices can be examined further after payment. This further examination can be performed in one of two ways. First the invoices can be further checked by internal audit; this would involve the internal auditor making examination of the invoice to check the following points:

(a)   that it was addressed to the authority and not to an individual by name;

(b)   that it carries the name and address of those who sent it;

(c)   that it is **not** a 'statement' or 'copy' but an 'invoice';

(d)   that the date relates to the period under review;

(e)   that the invoice refers to the goods or services ordered, the type and quantity ordered;

(f)   that all discounts offered have been taken;

(g)   that the invoice complies with standing orders and financial regulations.

The second means of further checking an invoice is a check performed by members. Not all members can be involved in a check but a small sub-committee may select a few invoices upon which the chief officers will have to report. The report will be presented by the chief officer of the spending department and the chief financial officer. Prior to making this report the chief financial officer will inevitably require the chief internal auditor to carry out a check by internal audit.

4.7   CENTRAL STORES

(a)   **Receipt of goods**

(i)   The storekeeper is the responsible officer for the receipt of all goods.

(ii)   It is in the storekeeper's duty to examine and verify the goods received for both quantity and quality against a delivery note.

(iii)   The delivery note should only be signed after completing the above steps. Damaged or inferior goods should not be signed for.

(iv)   The storekeeper should arrange for immediate transfer into a secure storage area.

(v)   Check the delivery note against the copy order and note the quantity of goods received and date on the copy order.

(vi)   The storekeeper should complete a stores received note and forward a copy to the purchasing officer.

(vii)   The receipt of the goods should be entered onto the appropriate stock record, usually a bin card.

(b)   **Issue of goods**

(i)   The storekeeper is the responsible officer for the issue of goods from store.

(ii)   The storekeeper should only issue goods from store upon receipt of an official stores requisition note signed by an authorised officer.

(iii)   The stores requisition note should be thoroughly checked by the storekeeper in terms of the date, cost code, quantity, quality and purpose of the goods to be issued.

(iv)   The stores requisition note should be signed by both the storekeeper and the person receiving the goods. This is an essential part of internal check.

(v)   The issue of the goods should be immediately recorded on the stores record eg, the bin card.

(vi)   A copy of the requisition note should be forwarded to the management accountant who will charge the appropriate cost centre with the value of the goods issued.

(c)   **Stock levels**

(i)   It is the storekeeper's responsibility to maintain a balance between the cost of carrying goods in stock against the costs of not carrying stock. Too much stock ties up capital whilst too little stock can result in an inability to meet service department demands.

(ii)   Prior to each financial year the storekeeper should establish the estimated annual demand for various items of stock.

(iii) Economic order quantities should be established for each item of stock. The economic order quantity is that amount of stock to be ordered each time a normal order is placed; it is the quantity of stock which minimises the total cost of holding stock and placing an order.

(iv) The economic order quantity is established by reference to the cost of storage space, the annual demand for stock, the cost of placing an order for stock and the cost of the goods themselves.

(v) Reorder levels for each item of stock should be established by the storekeeper. This is the level when an order is to be issued.

(vi) The factors to be considered in establishing a reorder level include the annual demand for stock, the economic order quantity and the time taken to replenish stock levels by the supplier.

(vii) All stock levels should be subject to regular review by the storekeeper.

(viii) The storekeeper would establish a system for regularly checking actual stock levels against the stock records.

4.8 BLAKESHIRE REGIONAL HEALTH AUTHORITY

From: Accounting Technician   Date: . . . .

To: District Finance Officer   Ref: . . . .

Establishment of joint use facilities

Background

The purpose of this report is to examine a proposal from the Regional General Manager that District Health Authorities give consideration to establishing joint use facilities for central purchasing and storage. This report is a preliminary examination of the general factors to be considered when appraising joint use facilities. The second part of the report considers the details which might be included in any contract on joint use. The report does not examine the pros and cons of central purchasing as this is a different issue.

General factors

Whatever the reason is for establishing joint use facilities the following points will provide a brief checklist to assist any decision.

(a) The arrangement should result in economies of scale because of cooperation in the acquisition and deployment of resources, eg, discounts on bulk purchasing and/or rationalising staff and building needs.

(b) The policy and operations of the joint facility should be capable of guidance and development by members and officers of all the constituent authorities.

(c) The effectiveness of the service provided should not be diminished by establishing the facility; it would be hoped that the quality of service to the authority and the public should improve.

(d) Because of the cost of and restrictions on capital expenditure, joint use facilities should not generate large amounts of capital payments, the use of existing buildings and equipment should be maximised.

(e)   Overall the benefits of the joint use facility should exceed the drawbacks of establishing such an arrangement.

Content of the legal contract

The financial issues to be included in the contract would include:

(a)   the cost sharing basis between member authorities;
(b)   the reimbursement arrangements for authorities incurring expenditure;
(c)   the accounting arrangements for the income and expenditure;
(d)   the audit arrangements, both that of internal and external bodies;
(e)   the budget preparation and budgetary control arrangements.

Other more general points for inclusion would include:

(a)   the policy making and management arrangements of the joint–use facility;

(b)   the length of time the contract is intended to operate for before renewal;

(c)   the relationship of member authorities, eg, is one authority the principal or are all members equal partners.

Summary

The initial suggestion is worthy of further consideration at the July meeting of District Finance Officers when the above issues can be developed.

4.9   CASHFLOW MANAGEMENT

(a)   Funds carried in the form of cash in hand or at the bank is just as much the employment of such funds as if they were locked up in stocks. The objective of cash management is therefore to minimise the amount of funds locked up in cash. The aim is to have the cash coming in matching the cash being paid out and with no cash in hand. The cost of holding cash is the profit that could have been earned or the service that could have been provided had the funds been put to another use. Thus the management of cash will require the calculation of the maximum cash commitment over the forecast period to determine the extent this can be met out of current receipts, or whether it will be necessary to employ short–term or long–term borrowing or lending. Thus cashflow management, if it is effective, will result in the following benefits:

(i)   Allows sufficient cash resources to be available to meet regular payments to employees, creditors and investors.

(ii)   Facilitates the planning of the timing and level of additional cash resources required to meet temporary cash deficits.

(iii)   Maximises the interest that can be earned by investing cash surpluses of the local authority. Conversely it will minimise the interest paid on long– and short–term borrowings.

(iv)   Ensures that debts are collected quickly, stocks are kept at appropriate levels and that creditors are paid at the appropriate time. Thus cash management aids the management of the authority's working capital.

(b) Public authorities are paid by various methods, four of which are illustrated below.

(i) **Cheque.** This method provides the authority with safety against loss or theft of cash. The making of the cheque 'account payee' increases this security as the cheque is not transferable or negotiable. Receipts need not be sent to the debtor thus saving administrative time and postal charges. The cheques have to go through the bank clearing system which can mean the authority does not receive the benefit of the funds until three or four days after the cheque is received. Cheques also can be returned by the drawer's bank because the cheque is incorrectly made out or because there are insufficient funds in the debtor's bank account. This will result in the authority losing the use of funds and having to follow up returned cheques with the debtor.

(ii) **Direct debits** are where the debtor presents a written instruction to their bank allowing creditors to withdraw monies from their bank account as and when debts fall due. The advantage to the authority is that the debtor does not specify the amount and thus differing amounts can be requested, eg, interest on mortgages. There are obviously costs and time involved in setting up the initial mandate but once this is done receipts can be more accurately predicted. This will assist cash planning for the authority. One weakness with this method is that the direct debit may not be actioned by the debtors' bank if there are insufficient funds in their account.

(iii) **Standing orders** are similar to direct debits in that they allow the debtor to make regular payments to the authority via the banking system. The principal difference is that the amount to be debited is fixed and cannot be varied other than by the debtor. Thus the method is useful for collecting regular debts of a fixed amount but it is less appropriate for fluctuating debts.

(iv) **Credit cards** are a popular and easy means of settling debts, whilst not accepted by all public authorities they are used in the more commercial parts of the public sector, eg, electricity bills, civic restaurants and theatres, airports, etc. The authority has no cash security problems and receives the credit immediately the debt is requested from the credit card company. Obviously the service has to be paid for by the public authority paying a fee to the company.

Similarly the authority will incur costs in introducing the system in terms of training employees. Overall as credit card usage is increasing authorities which offer this facility will perhaps enhance their image in the eyes of the general public.

4.10 REGULATIONS

(a) Ten principal procedures usually covered by the financial regulations of a district health authority comprise:

(i) production of annual accounts and reports;
(ii) control of stores;
(iii) security of cash, cheques etc;
(iv) security of information and data processing procedures;
(v) patients' property;
(vi) security of assets;

(vii) contracting and purchasing;

(viii) payment of staff;

(ix) estimates, budgets and budgetary control;

(x) internal audit.

(b) This answer will list instructions for **two** procedures as outlined below.

(i) **Payment of accounts**

1 The Treasurer shall be responsible for the prompt payment of all accounts.

2 All employees shall inform the Treasurer promptly of all monies payable by the Authority arising from transactions which they initiate, including contracts, leases, tenancy agreements and other transactions.

3 The Treasurer shall be responsible for designing and maintaining a system for the verification, recording and payment of all amounts payable by the Authority. The system shall provide for:

(a) certification that:

(i) goods have been duly received, examined, are in accordance with specification and order, are satisfactory and that the prices are correct;

(ii) work done or services rendered have been satisfactorily carried out in accordance with the order; that where applicable the materials used were of the requisite standard and that the charges are correct;

(iii) in the case of contracts based on the measurement of time, materials or expenses, the time charged is in accordance with the timesheets, that the rates of labour are in accordance with the appropriate rates, that the materials have been checked as regards quantity, quality and price and that the charges for the use of vehicles, plant and machinery have been examined;

(iv) where appropriate, the expenditure is in accordance with regulations and that all necessary authorisations have been obtained;

(v) the account is arithmetically correct; and

(vi) the account is in order for payment;

(b) a timetable and system for submission to the Treasurer of accounts for payment – provision shall be made for early submission of accounts subject to cash discounts or otherwise requiring early payment;

(c) instructions to staff regarding the handling and payment of accounts with the Finance Department.

4 Where an employee certifying accounts relies upon other employees to do preliminary checking he shall, wherever possible, ensure that those who check delivery or execution of work act independently of those who have placed orders and negotiated prices and terms. He shall satisfy the Treasurer as to the effectiveness of these agreements.

(ii) **Inventories**

1 Each employee has a responsibility to exercise a duty of care over the property of the Authority and it shall be the responsibility of Managers in all disciplines to apply appropriate routine security practices in relation to NHS property. Persistent breach of agreed security practices shall be reported to the District General Manager.

2 The District General Manager shall define the items of equipment to be controlled after receiving the Treasurer's advice and, wherever practicable, items of equipment shall be marked as Health Authority property.

3 A register of items to be controlled shall be maintained. The form of the register and the method of updating and of writing off shall be agreed by the Treasurer. All items in the register shall be subject to periodic independent check.

4 The items on the register shall be checked at least annually by the Unit General Manager or designated employee and all discrepancies shall be notified in writing to the Treasurer who may also undertake such other Independent checks as he considers necessary.

5 Registers shall also be maintained and receipts obtained for:

(a) equipment on loan; and
(b) all contents of furnished lettings

6 Any damage to the Authority's premises, vehicles and equipment, or any loss of equipment or supplies shall be reported by staff in accordance with the agreed procedure for reporting losses.

7 On the closure of a unit, a check shall be carried out and a responsible employee will certify a list of items held showing eventual disposal.

4.11 PAYROLL

Financial regulations relating to the payment of staff should include the following points:

(a) Approved establishment numbers, indicating maximum employable staff, must be observed by all managers.

(b) All new employees will receive a contract of employment and complete a signed appointment form. These will be sent to the Director of Finance.

(c) Similarly when employees leave the organisation for whatever reason, eg, retirement or resignation, the relevant documentation should be completed and forwarded to the Director of Finance.

(d) The Director of Finance shall initiate and approve all pay records and require that they are authorised by the approved officer.

(e) The calculation of pay is the responsibility of the Director of Finance. This will involve preparation of payroll data, income tax, superannuation, social security, etc.

(f) The methods of payment – cheques, bank credits or cash – shall be decided by the Director of Finance. This will include payment dates.

(g) Periodically physical checks of individuals may be made to see that they exist and also that they are receiving the correct wage/salary.

(h) Cash payments should be strictly controlled in terms of security, identification of recipient and also returning of unclaimed wages.

(i) Internal check should be established in that the cashier disbursing the wages should not be the person who calculates and makes up the wage packet.

(j) There should be regular and independent reconciliation of payroll control accounts; this is an essential control device and also facilitates internal check.

(k) Current pay agreements and conditions should form the basis of payment of salaries/wages; these could be local or national pay agreements.

4.12 IMPREST

(a) Small–value items are frequently purchased by organisations, usually out of a petty cash account; such items would include pens, postage stamps and local bus fares. Petty cash is drawn from the bank from time to time and disbursements are made for items of cash expenditure. The imprest system requires that all payments made from the account during the month are totalled at the end of the month, and the same amount of cash is put into the account as has been paid out during the month. These payments are analysed in the petty cash book and equate in total to the single entry in the main cash account. The above system is flexible and avoids having to raise cheques for small–value items.

(b) The following points would be included.

(i) A key role is played by the director of finance in authorising the establishment of petty cash accounts.

(ii) The use of an imprest system is required to control petty cash accounts.

(iii) Defined types and values for expenditure to be disbursed from a petty cash account should be prescribed.

(iv) All disbursements should be supported by signed disbursement vouchers giving the date of the transaction, the name of the recipient, the reason for the advance and the signature of the recipient.

(v) A petty cashier should be given responsibility for maintaining the petty cash records and the security of the cash.

(vi) The petty cash should be balanced monthly and topped up with an amount equivalent to the monthly expenditure incurred on petty cash disbursements.

(vii) The authority's auditors will have access to examine the records and system for maintaining a petty cash account.

(viii) No other income should be paid into the petty cash account other than the monthly replenishments of expenditure.

(ix) All items of expenditure should be analysed in a petty cash book over appropriate expenditure headings. There should also be information on the date of the transaction, the amount paid in, the voucher number, the amount spent and details of the transaction.

(x) Disbursements can only be made by the cashier who must sign every petty cash voucher supporting the disbursement.

4.13 CENTRALISED SERVICES

(a) Payment of creditors, preparation of the yearly financial accounts, investment management, internal audit, collation of the authority's revenue and capital budgets and preparation of the staff payroll.

(b) Economies of scale may result from centralisation. For example, preparation of one payroll rather than several payrolls requires less staff and computer time.

Staff who are responsible for the borrowing and lending of the authority's funds become specialists in particular areas. This improves the quality of service provided to the authority.

Centralisation assists financial control particularly via a central internal audit section. Common procedures and internal controls can be established and verified. Systems audits are easier to carry out as experience can be drawn from other departments.

(c) Floor area occupied would be used to recharge the costs of central buildings.

Actual or estimated time that architects spend on a particular job is a suitable method.

Personnel department costs could be recharged on the basis of employee numbers.

Job costing is appropriate for some larger printing jobs, whilst smaller photocopying facilities could recharge on the basis of unit costs.

(d) Recharging central services creates an internal market which will result in the efficiency and effectiveness of central services being questioned. This could lead to waste and inefficiency being reduced.

Including central costs ensures that such charges are fully reflected in the pricing of services in order to promote fair competition within the public sector and also between the public sector and the private sector. This is particularly important in competitive tendering processes.

0145V

Full cost principles are essential when claiming grants from central government, setting prices for use of services, making comparisons of unit costs, etc. To understate costs provides little incentive to use resources efficiently nor does it increase the awareness of public sector managers as to the true cost of providing services.

4.14 BANK RECONCILIATION STATEMENTS

(a) The objective of a bank reconciliation statement is to compare the cash book balance with that of the bank and to reconcile (ie, identify) the differences and analyse the variations between the two.

The following detail the general steps to be taken.

(i) The reconciliation should be undertaken as soon as possible after the end of each calendar month and should be completed by the 15th of the following month.

(ii) Obtain a copy of the bank statement as at the reconciliation date and balance the cash book to the same date.

(iii) Compare the cash book and bank balances on the opening day of the month to be reconciled. These will usually differ for reasons similar to those at the end of the month (eg, items in the cash book, not on the bank statement, such as unpresented cheques). Such differences will need to be identified and listed to be ticked off during the current reconciliation process. The important point is to be able to explain any opening differences in the two balances. The working papers of the previous month's reconciliation will assist in this task.

(iv) Compare the entries on the bank statement with the entries in the cash book since the previous reconciliation date.

(v) Entries that appear on both the bank statement and the cash book are to be ticked in red.

(vi) The unticked items will explain the difference between the two balances.

(vii) Enter in the cash book those items appearing on the bank statement but not in the cash book (eg, bank charges, direct debits, standing orders, direct credits). The correctness of these entries should be verified before entry into the cash book (eg, direct debits should be checked to the periodic payments register).

(viii) After all the relevant entries have been made, again balance the cash book and bring down the revised closing balance.

(ix) Check that all the items on the bank statement previously unticked have now been ticked. Any outstanding items should be investigated with the bank (eg, errors could have been made by the bank in making entries on the wrong account).

(x) Correct any errors found in posting the cash book (eg, errors of transposition).

(xi) Identify the items in the cash book that have not been ticked, eg, bankings made but not yet credited to the bank statement. These unticked items will be used to compile the reconciliation.

(xii) The bank reconciliation can now be prepared; it is normal to start with the balance per bank statement. The pro forma listed below should be used.

(b)   **Bank reconciliation pro forma**

Bank reconciliation for the month of 19XX

Prepared by . . . .   Approved by . . . .

Date of reconciliation . . . .   £   p

Balance per bank statement as at 31st 19XX
Add: Bankings made but not yet credited by bank:

Date	Details	Amount £ p
		—————— ——————

Less: Unpresented cheques

Cheque number	Payee	Amount £ p
		—————— ——————

Adjusted bank statement balance at 31st 19XX

                                                              ——————

Reconciled with

                                                                £   p

Opening cash book balance at 1st 19XX
Add: Total receipts per cash book for month

Less: Total payments per cash book for month   ——————

Adjusted cash book balance at 31st . . . . 19XX   ——————

                                                              ——————

4.15   PERSONAL COMPUTERS

(a) Eight items of information to be recorded on an employee file in a computer payroll system:

(i) employee name and date of appointment;

(ii) employee pay reference number which is unique to each employee and helps to minimise fraud and error;

(iii) income tax code and last date amended;

(iv) gross pay and deductions to date and also for the current period;

(v) rate of pay, overtime premium and any bonus payments in respect of this employee;

(vi)   details of deductions from salary (eg, trade union subscriptions) and the date deductions were authorised and period covered;

(vii)   departmental code to identify all the employee costs to a budget and/or cost centre;

(viii)   details of current employer contributions in respect of pensions and national insurance (these will be paid into the appropriate accounts).

(Noting the requirements of the Data Protection Act 1984.)

(b)   A computerised financial model is a hypothetical representation of the real world. It involves the simulation of reality thus enabling managers to play 'what if' analysis without incurring the expense of real decisions. Computers can therefore model reality utilising their capacity for large and diverse variables and speed of response.

The following are three examples.

(i)   An analysis of potential capital investment in fixed assets. The computer model could appraise options by quickly calculating the payback period, the net present value and the internal rate of return. The pattern of future cashflows and the discount rates could be amended to allow the technician to carry out 'what if' analysis. Thus by using a spreadsheet the technician is able to alter one value, say, the cost of borrowing, and the computer alters all the dependent variables automatically.

(ii)   Financial models using database facilities could be employed by the accounting technician to compile and maintain a fixed assets register. For example recent statutory requirements in the National Health Service require health authorities to construct and maintain a fixed asset register which allows the assets to be revalued and depreciated. The database model could be constructed to initiate this time consuming procedure automatically once initial values, scrap value, estimated asset lives, etc, had been input into the model.

(iii)   An accounting technician responsible for controlling the collection of debtors could use a database model to monitor debt collection. Thus a model of invoices issued could be matched against debtors paid via a common code. Thus it would be possible to display invoices issued by particular departments, to display debtors with bills outstanding over a certain number of days, sort the database into alphabetical or invoice value order, etc. Projections could be made as to levels of outstanding debtors to assist cash budgeting.

(c)   Five advantages of computer modelling would be as follows.

(i)   In setting a budget, numerous policy options may be considered (eg, the effect on running costs of gradually closing a long–stay mental hospital over several years).

(ii)   The routine clerical work associated with budget preparation can be both reduced and the arithmetic accuracy improved (eg, the implication of a change in national insurance contributions).

(iii)   The effect of alternative government policies may be examined (eg, the effects on revenue support grant to be received by an authority due to a change in the distribution formula).

(iv)   The use of a computerised financial model to produce a predetermined target, forecast or standard against which actual performance may be compared. Thus, a leisure centre may predict its expected revenues and clients on a monthly basis split over the various leisure facilities. This model can then facilitate budgetary control as the year progresses. Thus a greater range of options and detail is available when contrasted with the manual alternative.

(v)   A model clearly identifies the relationship between the various elements of the data. It also forces managers to recognise the inter-relationships. Thus a model could be built for a staff canteen which facilitates breakeven and profit-volume analysis. This would allow the relationship of changes in sales volume on profits to be seen. Key pieces of information such as the margin of safety and the breakeven point could be calculated to evaluate the implications of alternative courses of action (eg, pricing policy, menu choice, opening times).

4.16   WORKING CAPITAL

Capital is introduced into a business so that its financial requirements can be met (eg, stocks of goods for resale need to be purchased, fixed assets such as plant and vehicles are needed to run the business). The capital requirements of a business can be classified into fixed and working capital.

Fixed capital relates to the purchase of fixed assets, plant, buildings, machinery, etc. Working capital is the funding required to purchase current assets, which are continually circulating (ie, stocks, consumables, payment of creditors). When discussing working capital it is usual to do so by dealing with the topic of the working capital cycle (WCC). The WCC is essentially the outflow of funds spent on the purchase of stocks, etc, and the inflow of revenue received from debtors following the sale of the final product or service. WCC is often expressed in time, ie, the time it takes for the outflow of money to be replaced by incoming money.

It is very important that there is sufficient working capital at all times in the business. Under-provision will result in cashflow problems and the need to borrow. Over-provision means the business has money tied up that is not being efficiently and effectively used.

The WCC can be illustrated as follows.

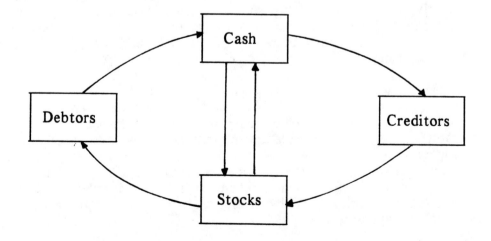

The public sector does not generally sell products; rather, it mainly supplies services, yet it still carries high levels of stocks. For example, hospitals carry stocks of drugs and dressing, local authorities have stocks of provisions, highway materials, stationery, vehicle parts, fuel, etc. The acquisition of the stocks all tie up cash (eg, creditors with to be paid promptly). Similarly the debtors of public sector organisations are mainly central government who provide grants, charge–payers and business owners who pay local taxes and the general miscellaneous debtors for goods and services provided on credit.

It is apparent that public sector organisations need to control each of the elements making up working capital. In particular it is necessary to recognise that there can be high costs associated with carrying working capital, namely the cost of borrowing. Stocks and debtors are cash tied up which is not available to pay staff and outside creditors. If each of the items – stock, debtors, creditors and cash – is considered it can be illustrated how effective management of working capital can benefit a public sector body.

Stock control is an important task and can bring benefits to, say, a local authority. The cost of holding stock includes such items as the stores personnel and running expenses, the risk of damage and obsolescence, interest charges paid on funds tied up in stock values, etc. If the local authority can establish economic order quantities, minimum and maximum stock levels, adequate stores control systems, etc, such holding costs can be minimised. Obviously the repercussions of not carrying adequate stock levels can have significant effects (eg, the lack of an important drug in an operating theatre).

The granting of credit to customers generates two main costs: (a) the administrative cost of collection and (b) the financial cost of borrowing funds temporarily or the opportunity cost of revenue that could have been earned had the customer paid in cash. It is critical that debtors be kept at the lowest possible level. It requires invoices to be raised as quickly as possible after the service has been supplied, that grant claims are submitted promptly, that community charge bills are sent out on time, etc. Similarly there needs to be an automatic follow–up of debtors and ultimately appropriate legal steps taken to recover the debt. The introduction of the community charge and the business rate has illustrated the financial costs to be saved when debtors pay promptly.

Goods and services are purchased by public sector bodies on credit. Control of creditor payments can bring benefits to the organisation by minimising the costs involved in taking credit. For example if a creditor offers a discount for prompt payment and this is missed it costs the authority funds. Suppliers may refuse to supply goods in the future, so disrupting services, if debts are not settled in a reasonable time. This should not discourage the use of credit for, if everything was paid for in cash there would be interest lost on the cash leaving the organisation.

Cash is a working capital item which if managed well will benefit the public sector organisation. The cost of holding cash will be minimised if cash is managed well. For example the costs of security, the risks of theft and misappropriation and the interest lost from possible investment or reduction of overdraft costs will be reduced by effective cash management. There are two aspects to cash management; firstly that concerned with cashflow planning and budgeting; secondly ensuring the cash resource is utilised effectively by controlling the authority's stock levels, by minimising debtors and by controlling the flow of creditor payments.

Cash budgeting entails identifying and quantifying the cashflows of the authority. These cashflows in a local authority will include salaries and wages, trade creditors, government grants, business rates, community charges, etc; many of these flows can be predicted with some certainty (eg, salaries and wages) whilst others such as debtors and community charges can be more erratic. It is now necessary to combine the cashflows in a daily, weekly and/or monthly cash forecast to determine the overall effect on cash balances. The authority will now be in a position to formulate its cash strategy. The forecast will reveal surpluses and deficits of cash in the future thus arrangements can be made to secure bank loans and/or overdrafts, to reschedule cashflows or to lend surplus cash on a short-term basis. This approach to cash planning when put alongside the management of stocks, debtors and creditors referred to earlier will provide the base for effective cash management. Of course cash plans need to be monitored on a daily basis to see that the actual cashflows are consistent with the plans; if they differ the reason has to be found and corrective action taken (eg, cash collected in departmental offices, schools, etc, might not have been banked promptly or there might be delays in issuing and following up debtors accounts).

Overall the management of the elements of working capital will reduce the costs associated with excessive levels of debtors, creditors, cash and stocks. If correctly managed these items will be available at the right time, in the right quantities to assist in the effective implementation of an authority's objectives.

5   CASE STUDIES

5.1   BRAMLEY

(a)   Unit labour costs should be considered. If possible, statistics relating to the contractors should be examined; both regarding wage rates and staffing levels.

(b)   Work design should be investigated. Gilbreth showed that the number of bricklaying motions could be reduced from 18 to 5. Perhaps the number of motions involved in refuse collection could be similarly reduced; for instance, by persuading residents to leave rubbish ready for collection in plastic bin liners.

(c)   Is the best available technology being used? If so, can its efficiency be increased?

(d)   Do the employees work well as a team? Group bonuses tend to help cohesion. Similarly, individual incentive schemes may help sustain individual motivation. In addition, formal appraisals could be introduced. At the very least, management should take the trouble to thank the refuse disposal officers for their services – feedback is essential.

(e)   Training should be introduced so that workers can take over each other's duties in emergencies – thus avoiding expensive contingency plans.

(f)   Perhaps the local government's management style is at fault? If so, extensive training (both by lectures and 'on the job' instruction) would prove invaluable.

(g)   If industrial actions (strikes etc) are frequent, then the management may attempt to remedy the situation with a more pluralistic approach to union relations. An improved position would be necessary to negotiate a more flexible working arrangement with the unions.

(h) If productivity is low, because of inherently unsuitable employees, management may consider:

  (i) whether a move to another department might prove beneficial; or

  (ii) whether recruiting procedures should be improved.

5.2 INDUCTION PROGRAMME

The existing style of management, or leadership seems to be effective as the team working on the systems development project have been operating very efficiently. As the new leader, John Newby will bring different managerial qualities with him, and possibly because of this may not find it quite so easy to run things as they have been done for the last two years. Before briefing him on the job it will be necessary to find out whether he has had previous experience of leading a team. As he has been with the company for some years he probably has had. For these purposes it will be presumed that Newby has had previous experience. If he had not, it would have been necessary in the briefing to include a general discussion on how to lead a team. In this particular case the briefing will be about the team and project only.

Discussions on group effectiveness suggest that the following aspects should be considered when briefing a new leader of a team: the project itself; the group; the environment they are working in; and any other relevant factors.

The project

(i) Because John Newby has to take over in the middle of the project, he will have to be carefully filled in on the current state of progress. The project's aims and objectives will have to be explained, what developments have been made so far, the time scale of the project, what plans have been drawn up to complete the other phases of it, and what each member of the team has been working on together with the results.

The group

The new leader will have to be informed about each of the team member's personality and attributes, so that he will know what each can or cannot do, and how to treat them best.

He will need to know in particular:

(ii) What skills each one has. He will then be able to give each the most apt task to suit their abilities.

(iii) What the individual's interests are, and conversely their dislikes. The leader might then find it more effective to work with these likes and dislikes, rather than against them.

(iv) How each team member gets on with the others, so that the leader can if possible make arrangements for those who get on well to work together, and for those who do not.

(v) What their domestic situations are. This is important for example, if it is necessary to ask some of the team to work late or over weekends; single members would probably be more willing than those who are married.

(vi) What each member's attitudes and values are, in order to avoid hurting their feelings. For example, it would be better not to accuse someone who takes a great deal of pride in his job of bad workmanship, unless it was absolutely necessary to do so.

(vii) Whether there is an informal group leader, and so to work with that person; or if some members are more difficult to deal with than others.

Inter-relationships

(viii) Any group characteristics or practices which have been developed will have to be made known to the new leader, so that he can make optimal use of them. For example, the team members may have evolved certain ways of operating, a particular manner of meeting, and ways of co-ordinating and reporting their tasks which suit them and which it is probably better not to change. Alongside this information the new leader should be informed about how well the team gets on with other groups and departments. Physical factors, such as where the team prefer to work, and how they like any equipment they have arranged, should also be considered here.

Other relevant factors

(ix) Style of management could come under this heading. Although the new leader will have his own style, the style which worked well in the past should be mentioned. The nature of the project will also indicate what sort of style would be best – whether informal or authoritarian, etc.

(x) Finally, the new leader should be briefed on procedures and tasks in the project – what standards are required and how to meet them, how to motivate the group, who does what job etc.

This is not an exhaustive list and other reasoned points may be included.

5.3 LOCAL AUTHORITY

Five possibilities are given for illustration, although only **four** are required for the answer.

Staff morale and productivity may have dropped as a consequence of the change of managers for several reasons.

However, it is difficult to comment in detail because of the lack of personal information provided about the new manager, it may be simply that he gets on with the employees as badly as the previous manager did.

(a) There has not only been a change in manager, but also a new system of organisation introduced. The head of each section now has to report to two assistant managers, one for administration and the other for public contact, rather than directly to the manager himself. It could be this change in system, rather than the new manager per se, which has caused the problems. The more complex structure of authority may have caused some perplexity and uncertainty among the section heads. Because the length of the chain of command has been increased, the staff may well feel that they are now a far lower part of the organisation, and so less significant and important – merely cogs in a machine. This would probably cause them to feel less a part of the organisation, and so their previous loyalty and commitment to the local authority would decline.

(b) Weekly performance reports and briefing meetings have also been instituted. This could easily have annoyed and caused resentment among the professional members of staff who previously had just got on with their jobs, and who probably valued their personal responsibility and autonomy highly. They could take umbrage at being briefed on what to do, feeling that their own judgement was all that was necessary in the past and that a system of formal reporting on performance shows that the manager does not trust them to do their jobs well. They may also think that the new manager does not feel that the work they had done in the past was up to a satisfactory standard. In short, such checks would hurt their professional pride.

(c) The new manager's business–school background may be a cause of the problems being experienced. The staff may feel that he is more interested in creating an 'ideal' business system than in providing the type of service to the public which, under his predecessor they had done.

This suspicion would be borne out by the institution of the new organisational and working practices of the new manager. This idea that what is important to them is no longer regarded as so by the manager could make them feel that their work as a whole is undervalued in the new system. This would result in a loss in morale and a lack of commitment to their jobs. It would also explain the decline in outside activities, because these too would be felt to be unimportant in the new system, and so there would be the feeling of why put effort into doing them when they now do not seem to matter.

(d) Because of the longer chain of command, due to the two new assistant managers, the staff may feel that the new manager does not really communicate with them as the previous one did. The old manager may have had an unpleasant personality, but he did notice the performances of each of his staff and personally commented on them, which gave regular, thorough, but fairly informal feedback to each employee on how they were doing. This did show that the manager was interested in each individual, as themselves and as part of the team, which certainly seems to be lacking under the new regime. It also shows that he thought that each person's contribution was important and worth remarking on. The staff may now feel that their work does not really matter any more.

(e) The previous manager was not only disliked by his staff because of his personality but also by his own superiors. This probably meant that there was not a good working climate in the organisation, but it may have brought some advantages. It would have weakened the authority of the manager, and so his staff would have had more autonomy and responsibility for their work, which would have boosted job satisfaction. The manager's unpopularity could also have created a cohesiveness within his staff based on a common dislike of him, and also possibly a fellow feeling between he employees and the manager's superiors as the superiors also disliked him. This would now be missing. Indeed if the new manager got on well with his superiors the opposite could be true of relations between the staff and senior management.

5.4 CHARLES

Rodger's seven–point plan is a technique for comparing a candidate's personal attributes with those required for a particular job. The plan attempts to provide a comprehensive system for assessing a candidate's suitability (or otherwise) for a particular position. Relevant to Charles, the seven–point plan may be applied as follows.

(1)   **Physical makeup**

Job requirement – Must be healthy, insofar as extensive travel is involved.

Charles' attributes – In good health.

(2)   **Attainments**

Job requirement – Specific technical qualifications.

Charles' attributes – Satisfied.

(3)   **Intelligence**

Job requirement – Reasonable degree of intelligence.

Charles' attributes – (Possibly) good to high intelligence.

(4)   **Aptitudes**

Job requirement – Sufficiently motivated to work by himself, and to be accurate in the technical aspects (eg, gauge reading).

Charles' attributes – Satisfied.

(5)   **Interests**

Job requirement – Travelling.

Charles' attributes – Domestic concerns, family matters, darts team, amateur dramatics; clearly a deviation from the ideal candidate.

(6)   **Disposition**

Job requirement – Ideally a loner, as he would have to work alone for extended periods.

Charles' attributes – Apparently very sociable, deeply entrenched in his community; a definite mismatch here.

(7)   **Circumstances**

Job requirement – The **ideal** candidate would be single, and have weak domestic ties.

Charles' attributes – Clearly unsuitable in this respect. However, Charles' circumstances include his having cashflow problems, which this job would help to rectify.

Conclusion

Charles' interests, disposition and circumstances render him unsuitable for the position. Behavioural theories all require that employees will only perform well if their own basic needs are met.

Maslow describes social and 'esteem' needs, McClelland describes motivation factors which, in this case, would not be satisfied.

Time allowed: Three hours

Number of questions on paper: Six

Answer **four** questions only

All questions carry equal marks

Where the terms 'organisation' or 'public sector organisation' are used, they are intended to refer to any part of the public sector unless there is a specific indication to the contrary in the question.

Where the question asks for an example in a public sector organisation of the candidate's choice to be given, the type of public sector organisation should be stated.

1   **AGENCY ARRANGEMENTS**

(a)   Identify and explain the reasons why a local authority would make agency arrangements with another public sector organisation.   (15 marks)

(b)   What problems and practical points could arise from such an agreement?
(10 marks)
(Total 25 marks)

2   **WAGES**

(a)   The payment of wages and salaries in cash carries major disadvantages. What are they?   (15 marks)

(b)   How can wages be paid other than in cash?   (10 marks)
(Total 25 marks)

3   **POLICY–MAKING**

Describe the process of policy–making in a public sector organisation, focussing upon the complexities involved.   (25 marks)

4   **PURCHASING PROCEDURES**

(a)   What procedures are followed in an organisation for the ordering of goods and their payment?   (16 marks)

(b)   What is a petty cash imprest? How does it work?   (9 marks)
(Total 25 marks)

5   **CORPORATE MANAGEMENT**

(a)   What is the purpose of corporate management in a public sector organisation?
(8 marks)

(b)   Examine the role and functions of a policy and resources committee within the corporate management approach.   (17 marks)
(Total 25 marks)

6   **FINANCE DEPARTMENT**

(a)   What are the functions of a finance department in a public sector organisation?   (15 marks)

(b)   What are the duties of the Chief Financial Officer?   (10 marks)
(Total 25 marks)

1 AGENCY ARRANGEMENTS

(a) The 1974 local government reorganisation in England and Wales prompted local authorities to make agency arrangements a common practice.

A major reason for the making of agency arrangements was to facilitate the changes embodied in the 1974 Act. By making agency arrangements the local authorities were able to maintain full employment for those staff in the functions they had lost such as water and highways. The agency arrangements also meant that all the back–up facilities could be utilised. Also similar agency arrangements were common for the provision of technical, financial and legal services.

Another reason for making agency arrangements lies in the fact that they assisted the development of the 'old' authority into its 'new' role.

It is also important to note that agency arrangements carry a number of advantages and therefore, although some of the earlier agency arrangements have been terminated, many have been maintained and new ones negotiated. An important advantage is that the agency allows the principal authority to use the facilities and services of the agent without the need for expensive duplication of provisions. A second advantage common to all agency arrangements is that they help facilitate a maximisation of benefits of scale. This will include such features as joint purchasing arrangements or perhaps the joint use of computer facilities.

(b) Agency arrangements **can** bring practical problems relating to the fair apportionment of costs but it must be noted that local authorities are well experienced in apportioning shared costs between different users and therefore agency arrangements should present no greater problems on cost sharing for a local authority.

A second, perhaps more difficult problem to overcome, is the determination of clear lines of authority. For example, to whom does the chief engineer, employed by a district council, but working on a county council project, report?

The viability of the agent's organisation is often maintained by agency work but the agent must be careful to ensure that the work pressures from the principal authority do not put his independent work under threat. The agency arrangements should operate to the mutual satisfaction of both agent and local authority. Provision should be made in the contract to allow the principal authority ready access to the agent's accounts in order to verify the basis and accuracy of charges. This provision may not be included, however, where the charge is fixed at a 'contract rate' rather than on 'reasonable actual basis'.

2 WAGES

(a) The Payment of Wages Act 1960 gives certain employees the right to demand payment of wages in cash, but payment in cash carries two major disadvantages as follows.

(i) Cash payment presents considerable security problems by the very presence of large and concentrated amounts of cash. Special security precautions need to be taken such as the employment of a security firm, the installation of security devices such as burglar alarms etc, and attendant costs for insurance premiums for cash in transit policies and fidelity guarantee cover.

(ii) Cash payment has a major drawback in that it is bulky. When thousands of pounds are being paid out as wages the sheer volume of the money is considerable. Consequently the cash payment will involve significant costs first in getting the money together and then in dividing the total volume into individual pay packets and then transferring these to individual employees.

Both the provision of security and the fact that wage payment involves considerable bulk, create significant costs. In addition cash wage payment imposes a peak load burden on administration; the payrolls operate to a tight schedule and often their final preparation involves overtime working to ensure completion within the time-scale.

(b) There are a number of ways in which wages can be paid other than cash. Perhaps the most common alternative is payment by cheque. A more sophisticated development of this is payment by direct bank credit which eliminates the risk of the employee losing the pay cheque.

This alternative and others similar to it require that the recipient has a bank account. On this point it is interesting to note that only about half of the adult population in this country does have a personal banking arrangement.

One further alternative non-cash method is the use of money orders. Such a form of payment is, however, very expensive for the employer and therefore unlikely to be preferred by him on a regular basis as opposed to cash payment.

3 POLICY-MAKING

Policy-making in a public sector organisation is not a straightforward process. The fact that there are different types of local authority varying in size, traditions, political views and all filled with people with different ideas and opinions is bound to add to the complexity of policy making.

There is no one way of policy making but most authorities follow a model similar to one of the following:

(i) 'Muddling through' – this is basically policy making in response to problems as they arise.

(ii) 'Incrementalism' – this is perhaps the most common model and involves making policy changes in small pieces. This model accepts the existing programmes of activity but does have a positive move for change as its objective.

(iii) The 'rational' is the most complete model as it considers needs, sets objectives, costs alternatives, implements and then reviews the policies made. Although it is an expensive and complex model it should foster a more efficient and effective use of scarce resources.

The policy-making process is also made more complicated by the diversity of services which a local authority operates and the competition for limited resources.

Finally, many groups both inside and outside the authority seek to influence its policy-making. This very fact makes policy making so much more complex. Those seeking to influence policy are numerous and include the following:

Inside the authority

(i) The chief officer of the department involved in the policy-making decision;

(ii) other chief officers who are competing, perhaps, for limited resources;

(iii) the chief financial officer who is concerned with external and internal constraints on finance;

(iv) the staff associations and unions within the authority who wish to influence policy on behalf of their members.

Outside the authority

(i) Other public authorities;

(ii) the media – their influence is felt through documentary programmes, articles, letters etc;

(iii) the government – it can influence policy making through its numerous controls;

(iv) the general public – through individuals, pressure groups, user associations etc.

4   PURCHASING PROCEDURES

(a) The procedure which is followed for ordering goods needs to be on a sound basis if the payment procedures are to be effective. The ordering procedure consists of a number of important control points.

The first control point is that an order **must** be covered by an approved estimate or a special financial provision before it can be issued. Second, the issue of an order can **only** come from a chief officer or someone nominated by a chief officer. The chief financial officer must also be informed of any person so nominated. The third control point is that orders must be made on official order forms. Recurrent expenditure on items such as rates, rent, heating bills etc does not require order forms. Fourth, if an emergency precludes order forms etc then the order can be made verbally but it must be confirmed within a day in writing on an official order form. Any amendments to an order must be entered on a duplicate copy of an order form by the chief officer or his nominee. Finally, each order must conform with the directions of the authority with respect to central purchasing and the standardisation of supplies and materials.

The procedure for making payments is standard, involving the following stages:

(i)   requisitioning goods;
(ii)   ordering supplies;
(iii) receiving supplies;
(iv)   receipt of suppliers' invoice;
(v)   certification of invoice;
(vi)   processing invoices for payment;
(vii) arranging the security and custody of cheques;

(viii) despatch of cheques;
(ix) internal check and internal audit.

(b) Petty cash is required to pay for small items, for two reasons:

(i) it is convenient and quick; and
(ii) it cuts costs which are incurred in making a payment by cheque.

The imprest system is the standard system for the operation of petty cash and it works in the following way. First, each department is given a lump sum which is to act as its petty cash for a certain period of time. The amount of petty cash payment is fixed and also the use of petty cash is limited.

Authorised vouchers must be presented when a claim for reimbursement is made. All unused cash should be kept in the office safe and receipts and payments must be recorded in a petty cash book. At the end of a month all vouchers paid should be submitted, with a summary sheet showing expenditure codes to be debited, to the finance department for reimbursement. Finally, at the end of the period for which the lump sum was supposed to last, a cheque will be received by the department for the amount of petty cash it has used during that period thus bringing the imprest to its original amount.

5 CORPORATE MANAGEMENT

(a) The concept of corporate management evolved during the 1960s but only became a reality in the 1970s. Its application to the public sector aimed to create interdependence between departments rather than the existing independence. The overall objective being to create a coordinating unit for policy making and effective use of resources. In order to achieve this a corporate management team is needed.

(b) The policy and resources committee is part of the management team. In the view of the Bains Committee the Policy and Resources Committee should 'have ultimate responsibility under the Board for the major resources of the authority, finance, manpower and land'. The committee then works to reconcile the desire to plan and expand services with the resources available to the authority. In this way the policy and resources committee has an important role to play in the internal financial control of the authority.

As the committee has 'ultimate responsibility' for the resources of an authority it should be involved in all aspects of the resource operations of the authority. It should encourage a corporate approach so that competition for resources is eliminated and departments adopt a corporate view. The committee also co-ordinates the plans of the various committees and the resources available to carry out such plans.

The above responsibilities and functions of the policy and resources committee are quite general; on a more detailed level the role of the committee will also include such tasks as the control and management of the authority's finances; the reviewing of fees and charges of the authority; supervising the collection and recovery of income; insurance arrangements, personnel and manpower planning; the purchase, sale and utilisation of land and buildings. Many of these activities are delegated to subordinate officers but the planning, co-ordination and control of these activities remains the responsibility of the policy and resources committee.

6 FINANCE DEPARTMENT

(a) The functions of a finance department vary considerably between one public sector organisation and another depending on the **type** of authority; the size and **functions** of the authority; the philosophy of its **members** and the philosophy of its chief financial officer.

The finance department exists for two main purposes; first to provide a service and second to provide control. the functions of the finance department can be classified under these two 'purposes'. The functions of a 'service' nature include paying salaries, paying bills, collecting **all** income, preparing **all** financial accounts and preparation of all cost and stores accounting for the authority. The financial department is also responsible for arranging all insurance cover, providing advice on financial matters, making all investments on behalf of the authority, co-ordinating the annual budgets to provide a total plan of resource allocation for the authority.

The functions of a 'control' nature are basically twofold. First the finance department is responsible for provision of an internal audit service. Second of the 'control' functions is the use of budgets and systems of standard costing for the purposes of control by comparing actual performances with the budget or a pre-determined standard. The objective of this is to achieve efficiency.

(b) The chief financial officer must perform a number of duties. He is responsible for maintaining an internal audit service for the whole authority. He also acts as a receiver and paymaster, collecting all the money owed to the authority, recording and banking the money. Another duty is that of preparing a comprehensive, centralised financial accounting service for the authority and supplying all necessary management accounting information to members and officers. A fourth duty is that of provision of financial advice to the authority including financial appraisals, reports on capital financing, etc. The Chief Financial Officer is also responsible for providing a comprehensive computer service to all departments of the authority.

An important duty of the chief financial officer is that of budgeting and budgetary control, ie, preparing budgets for revenue and capital expenditure.

The duties of the chief financial officer mirror the functions of the finance department which he heads.

1   It is important that the student refers to the 1974 local government reorganisation because the need to facilitate the changes brought by this Act gave the impetus to agency arrangements being made by the local authority. Since that time, however, agency contracts have come to an end and therefore the formation of new agency arrangements or the continuation of old need to be explained by reasons other than the 1974 local government reorganisation.

     The further reasons for making agency arrangements lie in the advantages to be gained by the local authority. Joint use of facilities is one advantage, an example of which is shared computer facilities.

     It is important that the student should be able to demonstrate an awareness and knowledge of the practicalities of operating an agency arrangement. Although apportionment of costs is a minor difficulty which a local authority should overcome, the determination of clear lines of authority is a more difficult problem. This kind of problem is resolved primarily by flexibility and common–sense on the part of the local authority and the agent.

     It is important to note the accessibility of the local authority to the accounts of the agent. Hopefully an agency arrangement will cut costs and create economies and therefore it is important that the local authority can check the accuracy and basis of the charges.

2   The payment of wages and salaries in cash has a strong tradition in this country, a tradition which affects current day attitudes towards cash pay days and a tradition which is supported by legislation. The major piece of legislation providing for cash payment is the Payment of Wages Act 1960 which gives certain employees the right to demand payment of wages in cash.

     The two major drawbacks of payment of wages in cash, security and bulk, are both primarily **cost** disadvantages. The special security precautions which need to be taken are costly whilst there is also a considerable cost involved in assembling such a large volume of money and in distributing the money accurately amongst the employees of the organisation. The fact that overtime work is often required in order to ensure that the payrolls operate to their tight schedule will also add to costs.

     The major alternative to payment in cash is payment by cheque. This form of wage payment means that cash need not change hands as the employer's bank account is debited and the employee's account is credited. To further eliminate any risk of mishandling wage payment direct bank credit may be used.

     It is important to note that only 50% of the adult population in England and Wales have a bank account. Local authorities and health authorities who make payments by cheque, especially to their own employees for wages and salaries, will have a considerable problem in that they have to allow encashment facilities, normally on the business premises. It can be noted that the issue of crossed cheques will provide added security for if the cheques are mislaid or stolen they can only be credited to the payee via the banking system. Finally, some local authorities have arrangements with major credit card companies so that wages may be received via the credit card.

3 The processes of policy-making in the public sector are extremely complex and in answering the question the student needs to show an awareness and understanding of the factors which make for this complexity.

The diversity within the organisation in terms of personnel and their views makes policy-making more complex. Also the number of different people within the organisation seeking to influence the policy should be referred to as a factor, noting also just who these people are. As well as those people seeking to influence the policy-making decision from inside the organisation there are groups and, in particular the government, outside the organisation which seek to influence the policy-making. The most influential of these is probably the government which can exert control over the public sector organisations through finance, its publications and even through ministerial statements.

It is important to focus on the policy-making models available to, and used by, the public sector organisations. These models assist the organisation in policy-making and making the most effective and efficient use of the available resources.

4 It is most important that the ordering of goods and their payment follow a set procedure to ensure that budgeted expenditure is not exceeded. If the procedure is followed then there can be control of ordering goods and control of expenditure.

The procedure provides for there to be official authorisation of any and every order. Except in emergencies all orders must be made in writing and approved by the chief financial officer or a nominee of the CFO.

The payment of bills received by the public authority is almost a continuous process and because it is a very important activity to ensure that the organisation operates in an efficient and effective manner, it is important that it is controlled by a set procedure. Once again each stage in the procedure must receive official authorisation if not from the chief financial officer then from another officer who has received the power of authorisation from the chief financial officer. Only periodic payments such as rates, rents, electricity charges, gas charges are exempt from having to make an official order. It must be noted, however, that since an official order is not issued a register of periodic payments should be maintained to afford control over such payments.

Every public sector organisation needs petty cash for the purchase of small items. Although payment of items with petty cash does not require official forms a record must be kept of all transactions involving petty cash. The imprest system provides for accurate records, and reimbursement of petty cash funds at the end of a fixed period.

5 A local authority was conceived as a single organisation with corporate objectives and plans for their implementation and not as a provider of a number of different services through independent and uncoordinated departments. The purpose of corporate management may be seen, therefore, as the means of fulfilling the above. It can do this because the nature of corporate management is to co-ordinate the activities, plans etc of the different departments, formulating a management team so that a corporate, ie, joint view of the organisation and its needs is taken and not a departmental or sectional one.

The policy and resources committee is part of the corporate management team. This committee is responsible only to the Board or Council and all other committees, individuals etc in the management team are answerable to and must report back all their activities to the policy and resources committee. The policy and resources committee is assisted by four sub-committees responsible for, respectively, finance, personnel, land and the performance of the organisation.

The policy and resources committee is responsible for numerous tasks, financial, personnel and manpower planning, land and buildings etc; many of these tasks are delegated to sub-committees but it is important to note that the responsibility remains ultimately with the policy and resources committee.

6   It is important to note the number of marks allocated to each part of the question and to allocate time spent on each part accordingly. Misallocation of time can lead to a loss of marks. It is also important to read the question carefully and answer the question which is set!

A public sector organisation cannot operate without finance; in order to use that finance efficiently, personnel with knowledge of finance and the ability to apply that knowledge to financial management and administration must be employed.

The finance department is responsible for all financial matters in an organisation. This includes paying salaries, collecting all income, paying bills, preparing financial accounts, arranging insurance cover, making investments etc.

The finance department also has duties of reporting and budgeting. This involves making annual reports for the board; also reporting to various committees. The budgeting is a vital function of the department. It is part of the 'control' function. Budgeting includes allocation and control of resources.

In part (b) it is important to make a mental note of the mark allocation. In order to gain the ten marks a number of points need to be made.

It is evident that the duties of the chief financial officer, who is the head of the Finance Department, reflect the activities of the department itself. The effectiveness of the chief financial officer in the performance of his task is critical to the effectiveness and efficiency of the finance department and of the organisation as a whole. The accounting, financial administration and control system of the local authority or organisation is the responsibility of the chief financial officer.

0147V